Parenting Kids

To Become the People Employers
Really Want and...

America Desperately Needs!

Charles Fay, Ph.D.

Parenting Kids

To Become the People Employers
Really Want and…

America Desperately Needs!

Love and Logic® PRESS Inc.

Charles Fay, Ph.D.

Love and Logic Press, Inc.
2207 Jackson Street, Golden, CO 80401-2300
www.loveandlogic.com
800-338-4065

LOVE AND LOGIC, LOVE & LOGIC, BECOMING A LOVE AND LOGIC PARENT, AMERICA'S PARENTING EXPERTS, LOVE AND LOGIC MAGIC, 9 ESSENTIAL SKILLS FOR THE LOVE AND LOGIC CLASSROOM, and 🔒 are registered trademarks or trademarks of the Institute For Professional Development, Ltd. and may not be used without written permission expressly granted from the Institute For Professional Development, Ltd.

Library of Congress Cataloging-in-Publication Data

Fay, Charles, 1964-
  Parenting kids to become the people employers really want--- and America desperately needs! / by Dr. Charles Fay.
     p. cm.
  ISBN 1-930429-96-7 (pbk.)
  1. Child rearing. 2. Parent and child. 3. Parenting. 4. Career education. I. Title.
  HQ769.F2325 2008
  649'.64--dc22

                           2008042742

Published and printed in the United States of America.

Table of Contents

ACKNOWLEDGMENTS

My thanks and praise must first go to the Lord. In times of trouble, You are my rock and my comforter. When I'm wise enough to listen, You always guide me along paths of goodness and love. Without Your great blessings this book would have never been written. Even though I'm just a man...full of faults...Your compassion never fails. It begins anew each and every morning.

Cody, my son, you are nothing short of a miracle. You make my heart leap with joy every time I look into your eyes. Seeing the world through your bright new eyes has taught me so much. The happiness you have given me has made writing this book far easier.

Monica, you are the woman of my dreams. How blessed I am to have a wife of such noble character. You are always forgiving of my faults. Your example and loving guidance have made me a far better man. Your encouragement and patience have made writing this book so much easier. I love you beyond words!

Mom and Dad, you gave me so many gifts. You always loved me for who I was...not who you thought I could be. You taught me to work hard. You taught me that I could do anything if I just worked hard enough. When I was a child, you laid down a foundation of courage that enabled me to spend the long and lonely hours required to write this book.

Thanks to all of you who still believe that raising children with character is the most important job in the world.

ABOUT THE AUTHOR

Charles Fay, Ph.D. is a parent, business owner, internationally acclaimed consultant, and author of numerous books, articles, audios, and videos. Educators, mental health professionals, and parents around the world have profited from his practical, down-to-earth solutions to the most challenging problems displayed by youth of all ages. These solutions come from years of research and experience serving severely disturbed youth in psychiatric hospital, public school, and home settings.

Dr. Fay has also developed an acute understanding of the personnel challenges faced by today's business owners and managers. Through his research and day-to-day experience managing employees, he has developed an intimate awareness of the types of employees bosses truly want...as well as how to find and cultivate them.

INTRODUCTION

We all want our children to grow up to be happy and productive adults. A key factor determining whether this dream becomes a reality is how well we prepare them for success in the workplace. Unless we have the resources to set them up with a life-long trust fund, our youngsters are going to spend most of their adult lives at work. The more skills we give them for success in the workplace, and in life, the happier they will be! Knowing what today's employers are looking for illuminates the types of attributes we're wise to help our kids develop. I've included the news article below because it gives us some wonderful clues. Immediately following the article is my response.

Businesses Adopting "Employee-Centered" Approach

By Kenton Clarkson
Finance Journalist
The Mountain Times and Reporter

A new wave is sweeping the world of big business. The power ties and strict work hours are coming off in favor of a friendlier, more progressive "employee-centered" approach. According to Louise Sands, President and CEO of Sands Astro-Tech, leaders of big business are finally catching up with recent research findings.

"We're finally starting to get it. It's not unusual for practice to lag behind research. Now we're beginning to understand what it takes to create a truly employee-effective business climate."

Jerry Rouse is playing an instrumental role in his company's emergence from the dark ages of traditional performance-focused management. "We're doing more than just talking about it," says Rouse, "We're taking the lead in the telecom industry by taking concrete steps to recognize and honor the diverse working styles of our employee family."

There's word on the street that all business sectors are responding. Sands comments, "If companies want to attract and keep key personnel, they need to shed their Neanderthal-like perspectives. It's time for a paradigm shift!"

So what's this shift look like for companies who've made the transition from Edsel to high-tech hybrid-powered employee management? TMT Manufacturing of Valley View has taken the following steps:

Desire-Based Work Hours

At the heart of the employee centered business model is a strong emphasis on employees choosing their own work schedules. Tammy, one TMT sales associate, commented on the big difference this has made in her life: "My old job was so lame. I had to be there every morning by 8 am, my lunch was only an hour, and I had to stay until 5! I love working at TMT because I get to choose what time I get there and how long I stay. It's really cool when I'm tired in the morning or when it's really nice outside and I feel like taking off early."

Code-Free Dress

At TMT employees aren't encumbered by the unrealistic dress codes so often found in less progressive workplaces. Sue, a receptionist, loves this asset. "It's the best! When I feel like wearing a tube top, I wear a tube top!"

Aspiration-Sensitive Time Centers

Jason Argonata, TMT Executive Personnel Manager, argues that a focus on diverse aspirations and motivational styles is critical: "At TMT we understand that employees' work orientations and desires are in a constant state of flux. That's why each is free to determine how they spend their time at any given moment."

Corey, recently hired by TMT, believes that all companies should follow suit: "It's awesome. When I get tired of doing something that's hard, I can go to another center where the task is better suited to my desires. If I don't like that center, I can keep trying others or just chill. Nobody gets on your case about it."

Performance Non-Contingent Compensation Structure

"It goes without saying that compensation structure has a huge impact on attracting and keeping the best and the brightest," says Argonata. "The TMT way recognizes that anxieties about performance-contingent pay and bonuses runs counter to the self-actualization process. Employees shouldn't have to bear the burden of worrying that their pay is linked to what they produce. This just creates too much stress."

Individualized Parent Involvement Plans (IPIPs)

"The benefits that parents can bring to the table are immense," says Sands of Sands Astro-Tech. "It's critical that parents are welcomed as equal members of the management decision-making team."

At TMT, each employee has an individually tailored IPIP designed to give parents plenty of opportunities to consult with management regarding their adult child's aspirations, unique work styles, and deserved compensation. Sales associate Wilma gives the IPIP concept a double thumbs up, "Every morning my mom sends my boss an email that gives him a heads-up on what I need. Then he sends her a progress report at the end of the day, outlining what he's done to help. I think it really helps him stay on track."

Wilma's co-worker, Kurt, is an even bigger advocate, "If it weren't for my dad's input at my last evaluation, there's no way I would have gotten that raise!"

Employees seem to love this new approach, but what about productivity and the all important bottom line? Rouse scoffs at the critics, "For decades, business leaders have gotten away with this sort of arrogant self-aggrandizement and myopic obsession with net income figures. The old guard has lost its edge and is too greedy to admit it."

According to Sven Bornboergenson of the International Association for Employee-Centered Workplaces (IAECW) this new approach is here to stay. That is, if there are enough qualified employees available to meet demand. Bornboergenson worries, "We've got big problems if parents, schools and universities don't step up to the plate by teaching skills marketable in this modern business milieu."

Due to these concerns the IAECW has issued a position statement outlining its recommendations to parents, public schools and universities for creating young adults ready to participate with success in the employee-centered workplace:

- **Make sure that children are never expected to struggle, wait or experience boredom.**
- **Never say words like "No," "I expect" or "chore."**
- **Teach them that limits and rules do not apply to them.**
- **Always rescue them from the consequences of their poor decisions.**
- **Let them frequently overhear you complaining about work and how unfair your boss is.**
- **Teach them that being happy is more important than doing what's right.**
- **Never grade their papers with red ink. Use a friendlier color that won't damage their self-concept.**
- **Increase the amount of time they spend watching TV and playing video games.**

While many believe that the employee-centered workplace is the wave of the future, others remain unconvinced. Dr. Charles Fay, an outspoken critic of the IAECW, argues that the world economy is better served when young people believe in the antiquated ideas of our forefathers. "Nobody wins when parents and schools produce kids who believe they are the center of the universe. A far happier result is achieved when youngsters are taught to ask, 'How can I serve others?' instead of 'How can others serve me?'"

The jury is still out. Will this new approach bite the dust like a house of straw blown down by the Big Bad Wolf of industry? Or will it thrive like a house of bricks? Only time will tell.

Okay! Now let's get real!

Obviously there's really no such thing as the "employee-centered" workplace described above…and all of the names included in the article were changed to protect the nonexistent. That is, except my own! This newspaper is a figment of my imagination.

I wrote this oddly believable piece of fiction not only as a psychologist, but as an employer and business manager. My motivation to pen this purely preposterous piece resulted from a troubling trend we've witnessed over the past three decades: ever increasing numbers of young people leaving home with habits and belief systems that set them up for success only in the mythical "employee-centered" workplace. Yes, we've had employees who believed that their parents had the right to dictate business policy on their behalf. Even scarier, some of their parents felt this way also! If you think we're alone, talk to some employers in your community.

Although it's human nature to find blame and focus on the gloom and doom, it's a far better use of ink and paper to zero-in on solutions. There's great hope for our children, our country, and our world! By taking a look at the upbringing of truly respectful, responsible, and happy adults, we can learn a lot. What do their parents do that dramatically increases the odds that they will become highly successful…and happy…employees? That's the focus of this book!

CHAPTER ONE

The Little Things Are the Big Things

Know the skills your kids need to succeed in the workforce.

Twenty-five-year-old Chris made a splash during the interview. His soon-to-be boss, B.C. Swiss, was dazzled by his resume. Hardly able to contain his enthusiasm, B.C. thought, "This kid's got it all! He's trained in advanced computer systems and finance. He's articulate, witty, well-dressed… the answer to my personnel woes!"

Chris was hired on the spot, and it didn't take long for him to demonstrate his advanced skills. As his resume promised, there were no computer calamities he couldn't calm, no balance sheet he couldn't balance. For Chris, hardware was no hassle, and software was a snap. Numbers were no problem, and machines posed no menace.

Despite this bliss, Mr. Swiss started seeing a few holes in Chris's performance. He appeared to be "punctuality-challenged." At first, he was just five or ten minutes late, once or twice a week. Then it became ten or fifteen minutes almost every day of the week. Despite his tardiness, he didn't think twice about asking for a raise during his one-month review.

There were other "small" problems…like making lengthy personal calls during work hours, playing computer games on company time, failing to show up for staff meetings, wearing ratty t-shirts and faded jeans, and annoying just about everyone in the office. Mr. Swiss wondered what happened to the clothes Chris wore to his interview. He also wondered why Chris refused to shape up when given a chance. Mr. Swiss didn't wonder about what needed to be done. Despite all of his wonderful technical skills, Chris was out of a job…and Mr. Swiss was searching for an employee.

Susie's resume was short. In fact, she'd worked for Mr. Swiss since she graduated with her Associate's degree from the local technical college seven years earlier. While a bit disappointed that Chris was hired for the position she secretly wanted, she couldn't blame Mr. Swiss. After all, Chris had all of the technical training that she lacked. Instead of complaining, she kept a stiff upper lip and did her best. As she'd always done in the past, she arrived a bit early every morning, she stayed a bit late every afternoon, she always tried to look her nicest, and she worked hard every minute of the day. She even made sure that no dishes went unwashed in the employee workroom!

As he drove home one evening, Mr. Swiss had a thought that made him smile. "What would happen if I gave Susie this job and allowed her to get some additional technical training? At least I wouldn't have to worry about her getting to work on time. I'd know that she'd make the best possible use of company time. She'd get along with the other employees. She'd be receptive to my feedback, and I wouldn't have to worry about her getting lazy."

Mr. Swiss learned what all smart bosses learn: It's far easier to teach someone the technical skills of their trade than the skills they should have mastered before their sixth birthday. These include how to…

- wait and take turns
- wash up and dress nicely when they leave home
- clean up after themselves when they make a mess
- listen and look people in the eye
- hold doors open for others
- say "please" and "thank you"
- follow simple directions and complete simple tasks without constant reminders
- stay calm when they're disappointed, frustrated, or angry
- employ basic table manners
- walk instead of run
- stand in line without hassling others
- etc.

By the first or second grade, they should also be able to…

- use an alarm clock and get themselves ready for school in a timely manner
- prepare a simple meal for the family
- clean up after that meal
- complete chores and other tasks without having to be nagged and reminded
- etc.

It's far easier to teach someone the technical skills of their trade than the skills they should have mastered before their sixth birthday.

Isn't it tragic that Chris…at the age of 25…lacked many of the skills listed above? Wouldn't it be great if he were a rarity? Wouldn't it be sweet if he was the only one? Sadly, employers… and college professors…are seeing more young adults who're so behaviorally and emotionally immature that they crash and burn when expected to perform in today's highly demanding and competitive work environment. It's the small things that trip them up. They may know their trade inside out, but they're lacking the basic "kindergarten skills" required for consistently performing their jobs in a responsible manner.

Yep! The little things really are the big things!

How are your kids doing so far? Are they mastering the skills that'll unlock the door to life-long success? Or will they suffer as others pass them by? If your kids are a bit behind in this area, there's good news. It's never too late to teach them. All it takes are the "Five E's" of Love and Logic:

- Example
- Expectation
- Education
- Experience
- Empathy

As this book unfolds, you will read many stories and examples of how parents have applied the five "E's" of Love and Logic to teach their children a variety of critically important skills and attitudes. You'll also see how these "E's" can save your daily sanity and lower your blood pressure!

June decided that she wasn't doing her twelve-year-old daughter any favors by running a personal taxi service for chronically tardy pre-teens. It started the first day of first grade, when her precious Patty slept late, needed endless help tackling her tangled hair, and couldn't find her favorite shoes...the ones that with little lights that flashed when she ran. They found her sneakers, but she missed the bus. "No problem," thought June. "She's just a little girl. I'll drive her to school." Years later "no problem" had become a "big problem." June was ready to experiment with a little Love and Logic.

The First "E" of Love and Logic: Example

June had tried all of the traditional tactics for getting Patty to be more responsibly speedy in the mornings. She'd lectured, threatened, begged, and bribed. Believe it or not, she'd even tried raising her voice! The harder she worked, the slower Patty seemed to move. Mr. Feta, June's boss, was an understanding guy, but he was getting sick and tired of hearing why she couldn't get to work on time. Sitting behind his desk, he peered over his reading glasses and said, "June, I'm sorry that you're having so much trouble with your daughter, but I've got a business to run. Your work is great, but I need you here in the morning to do it."

June wasn't surprised. "I know. I know. I'm at my wits end with her. Every morning it's hell. All I do is run around after her, trying to get her to hurry. I am so sorry."

"May I share a thought with you?" he inquired.

June trusted and admired old Mr. Feta. His many years of marriage, fatherhood, and grand-fatherhood had taught him a great deal about patience and compassion and how to bring the best out of people. "Sure," she replied.

"June, how is your daughter ever going to learn how to get ready on time if she isn't seeing you do it?"

Those gentle yet honest words smacked her over the head like a ten pound mallet. "He's right," she thought. "If I don't set an example, she'll never learn!"

As much as most of us hate to admit it, our kids will rarely behave better than we do. What a drag! I mean, wouldn't it be great if we could misbehave around our children? How wonderful it would be if kids could look at our bad behavior and reason, "Even though Mom and Dad are a bit 'responsibility-challenged' I choose better for myself. Fortunately, I was born with all of the requisite skills, attitudes, and wisdom to resist ending up like them!"

Our kids will rarely behave better than we do.

The first "E" of Love and Logic stands for Example...or modeling. Too frequently, in our desperate attempts to get kids to behave, we end up forgetting to display the behavior we want from them. Am I providing a good model when I raise my voice and lecture? How am I doing when I issue threats I could never back up? Are my kids seeing a solid model when my face turns red... or I give in to their demands?

At this point you may be thinking, "I knew that already. It's good and fine to spew about modeling, but how do I get my kids to behave? That's why I bought this dang book in the first place!" June was in the same jam. While she agreed with gray-haired Mr. Feta, she had no idea where to start. It's one thing to say it, but how do you do it? That's exactly the question she asked Mrs. Apple, the counselor at Patty's middle school.

The Second "E" of Love and Logic: Expectation

It wasn't the first time Mrs. Apple had met a mom with a chronically late kid, and it wasn't the first time she'd shared the same seeds of wisdom. "Do you really think Patty is old enough to get herself ready in the mornings and make it to the bus stop on time?"

June was more than a little surprised by this question. "Uh... well..."

"You don't sound too sure," Mrs. Apple prodded with a smile.

"Yes...I mean I think so. She's twelve, and I was doing it by the time I was six!"

"June," the wise counselor continued, "The reason I asked you that silly question was to see if you really expect that Patty can be responsible about such things. I've learned that our expectations have major effects on how our kids behave. Over the past twenty-some years I've seen how kids behave better for parents and teachers who communicate high expectations."

Mrs. Apple got right to the core of the problem!

Kids will either live up to...or down to...our expectations.

If June believes that twelve-year-old Patty needs to be nagged and taxied to school each day, so will Patty. In contrast, if she believes that Patty is capable of being far more responsible and independent, so will Patty. Each and every day, our expectations ooze out of us, easily spotted by our kids. If we're confident in their capabilities, the tone of our voice, facial expression, and posture will send a powerful "You can do it!" message. If we're not so sure, they'll be quick to get "You're not very capable!" messages instead. This is why Expectation is the second "E" of Love and Logic.

We also communicate our expectations by the types of limits we're willing to set and enforce. Parents who believe that their youngsters can learn respectful, responsible, and independent behaviors find it far easier to provide effective limits. Those who aren't so sure find themselves feeling far too guilty. Guilty parents rarely set meaningful limits with their children! If June truly believes that Patty can succeed, she'll experience little or no guilt when she says:

Patty, I will help you with your hair when I'm finished getting ready.

She won't be racked with remorse when she says:

Patty, my car is leaving at seven-thirty sharp.

And she'll have the guts to have her best friend show up at seven-thirty, ready and willing to say:

Patty, you missed the bus. That's sad. Your mom can't be late for work anymore, so I'm here to drive you...I charge fifteen dollars. Will you be paying me with cash or some of your things?

Do we really recommend doing something like this with a chronically late child? You bet! Would the friend really charge the child for driving them to school? Absolutely! When parents surprise their kids with this sort of approach, do their kids begin to take what they have to say a lot more seriously? There's no doubt!

Let's get back to our discussion on establishing high expectations by setting limits. What's more effective: issuing orders, or describing what you'll be willing to do or allow? What brings out the best in people? Telling them what to do...or describing what you will do? Can you really control the behavior of others? Or are your own actions and attitudes the only thing you can control? Love and Logic teaches a simple yet powerful rule:

Never tell a strong-willed child what to do. Instead, describe what you are willing to do...or allow...instead.

When we live by this rule, we apply "Enforceable Statements" instead of threats, lectures, or reminders. Listed below are some examples of Enforceable versus Un-Enforceable Statements. As you review these examples, consider the sorts of underlying messages sent by each. Also consider how each example relates to helping children develop the skills necessary for success in the workplace and in life.

Un-Enforceable Statement	Enforceable Statement
Hurry up!	*My car leaves in five minutes.*
Stop arguing with each other.	*I charge $2 per minute for listening to your arguing.*
You need to get a better attitude.	*I'll be happy to do the extra things I do for you when I feel respected.*
Take out the trash...now!	*I'll be happy to do the extra things I do for you when your chores are done.*
Go to sleep. You're going to be tired in the morning.	*In this house, everybody gets up by 6 AM, regardless of how late they stay up.*
Eat that!	*Dinner is served until 7 PM.*
Pick up your toys.	*The toys that you pick up, you get to keep.*
Drive safely!	*Feel free to drive the car as soon as you've made a deposit into my account equal to the insurance deductible.*
No! I'm not spending $200 on sneakers!	*I'll pay $40 toward those. If you can come up with the remaining $160 they are yours.*

Enforceable statements send "You can do it!" messages, and they result in more thinking and learning. Un-enforceable statements send, "You better do it!" messages and result in less thinking. They also lead to far more un-winnable power struggles. Enforceable Statements communicate high expectations. Un-enforceable ones send low ones.

Effective people never set limits over things they cannot control. As a result, they rarely find themselves feeling frustrated…and looking foolish…because they can't get their kids to do what they say. When we focus on our own behavior, we've got far more time and energy to model the skills we want our children to develop.

Effective people never set limits over things they cannot control.

Let's review. Up to this point, we've learned that…

- Ever increasing numbers of young adults are entering the workplace without the skills necessary for success.
- The skills they are lacking are not complicated technical skills but the basic behaviors typically learned during toddlerhood, preschool, and the early elementary grades.
- The first step toward teaching these skills involves modeling them.
- The second step involves truly expecting these behaviors by setting limits with Enforceable Statements.

What's the third step? June pondered this as she drove back to work from her meeting with Mrs. Apple. "I know Patty can be more responsible about getting herself ready on time. I know she can do it! I just haven't expected her to…or shown her how. If I'd started ten years ago, I wouldn't be in this fix!"

As she pulled into the parking lot at work, her thoughts drifted to another worrisome topic. "Today we're getting the new computers and software. This is not good! I just got used to the old ones, and I have no idea how these new ones work." Her legs moved just a bit slower as she walked through the doorway to her office.

The Third "E" of Love and Logic: Education

Mr. Feta said with a smile, "I bet everybody just loves the idea of having to learn a new computer system."

June thought, "Very funny."

He continued, "Brad, our I.T. guy will give you the education you'll need. He will sit down with each of you and give you step-by-step instruction. He'll start by showing you how he navigates the tool bars and commands, then he'll give you a list with the steps, then he'll give you an opportunity to practice on some sample data. As you practice, he'll be available to guide you along."

That day, June learned how to use her new computer...and a whole lot more. Brad the I.T. guy showed her how he used the new system, gave her some written guidelines, and sat by as she practiced. She noticed something about this young man. Whenever she ran into a problem and asked him what to do, he'd ask questions....instead of simply telling her what to do...

- *June, what do the guidelines tell you to do in this instance?*
- *Do you remember how I handled this problem when it came up for me?*
- *Which of these commands do you think would make the most sense here?*
- *How did you solve that problem earlier?*

A bit annoyed she asked, "Why do you ask all of these questions instead of just telling me what to do?"

Brad smiled. "Because folks forget what they're told but tend to remember what they figure out on their own."

As the afternoon passed, she realized that young Brad was wise beyond his years. People do seem to learn better when they have someone who guides them with questions…instead of just telling them what to do. She realized something else. She'd spent far too little time doing this type of education, or training, with her daughter.

It's easy to forget that kids aren't born with all of the basic skills and attitudes required to succeed in life. Most of us have been doing these things for so long that we can't remember ever learning them…but we did. Most of us have been doing them for so long that we can't remember anyone teaching us how… but someone did.

Are kids born already educated about the importance of saying "please" and "thank you"? Are they born knowing how to sit still, follow directions, talk quietly, and take turns? Do kids come out of the womb knowing how to get ready in the morning without missing the bus? At conception, are they automatically educated about the skills necessary for solving the problems life will surely throw their way? Nope!

The third "E" of Love and Logic stands for Education. If we want our kids to behave in certain ways, we have to teach them to behave in certain ways. Bosses rarely get excited about having to teach their employees how to take turns, share, clean up after themselves, etc. The earlier we start this education, the easier it will be for us and our children. But how do we do it? Brad the I.T. guy gives us some clues:

- He modeled the skills and described what he was doing.
- He provided some simple written steps for June to refer back to.

- He allowed June to practice using the program when the consequences of mistakes were still small (they used sample data).
- He watched, asked thoughtful questions, and allowed June to do most of the thinking.

If we want our kids to behave in certain ways, we have to teach them to behave in certain ways. Bosses rarely get excited about having to teach their employees how to take turns, share, clean up after themselves, etc.

Shelby is just two, but her parents think she's ready to start learning some basic table manners. Is it really possible to teach such a small tyke to dine with dignity? Shelby's mom and dad decide that it's best to start by modeling the behavior and talking about it with great excitement. Shelby's mommy says, "Look at this. I'm going to eat with my mouth closed!"

Later in the meal, Daddy pipes up, "I use my napkin instead of wiping my mouth on my shirt! See how I do it?"

Mommy replies, "Yes, and I also use my fork instead of my hands. See?"

The next evening, Daddy said, "Shelby! We're going to take some pictures of good manners tonight. Whenever somebody has good manners, we'll take a picture of them so that we can make a book!"

A couple days later, Shelby had a nice little book with pictures of her family using good table manners. It was fun to look at and talk about. It was even more fun to use when they were at the table. "Shelby, are you doing what's in the 'Good Manners' book?" Mommy asked. "Find the picture that shows us what you are supposed to do instead of using your fingers. Let's look together."

Like Brad the I.T. guy, Shelby's parents…

- modeled and described the skills they were teaching
- provided a simple visual guide for her to refer to
- allowed her to practice the skills when she was two instead of twenty-two…when the consequences of mistakes were still small
- involved her in the thinking by asking lots of thoughtful questions

Let's get back to June and her problem with Patty. If the four steps Brad the I.T. guy used apply to computer training, as well as teaching table manners, might they also apply to just about any other skill we're trying to teach? Saturday morning, June decided that it was the perfect time for her and Patty to start learning how to get ready on time.

Saturday morning? Why Saturday morning?

Like Brad the I.T. guy…and like Shelby's mommy and daddy… Mom figured that it was best for both of them to learn and practice a new skill when the price tag of mistakes was very low. Since there was nowhere they really needed to be on Saturday morning, being a bit late wouldn't be a problem!

"Patty," June asked her daughter, "would you like to go to the mall?"

Patty's ears perked, "Uh…yeah…that sounds good, Mom."

"Great! This will give us a nice chance to practice getting out of the house without any hassles."

A perplexed Patty mumbled, "Huh? What are you talking about? You are…like so weird."

Mom smiled, "I know. Unfortunately for you, a lot of kids grow up inheriting that trait from their moms."

Fighting back a smile, Patty countered, "What do you mean about practicing getting ready?"

"Well, Patty, you know how I nag you every morning to get ready for school? How would it be if I never did that again?"

"Yeah, right, Mom! Like you are going to stop nagging me? It's like your hobby."

June continued, "I need to apologize to you for treating you like a little kid every morning."

"Huh?" Now Patty was really confused!

"That's right," June smiled. "Starting tomorrow morning, I'm going to stop doing that."

"What?"

"Yes! From now on, Patty, I'm going to let you take responsibility for getting yourself ready on time. What do you think you will need to do so that you won't miss the bus?"

Patty's confusion gave way to annoyance, "Uh…like just get ready."

"That's true," her mother agreed. "But what will you need to do in order to be ready on time?"

"Uh…"

"Would you like some ideas?"

"Whatever."

"Patty, some kids decide to get organized the night before by setting out their clothes, packing up their books and homework, etc. How would that work for you?"

"I don't need to do that."

Resisting the urge to lecture, June kept on track. "Other kids decide to set their alarm clock really early so that they have plenty of extra time. Is this an option?"

"I hate getting up early."

"I know. Some kids decide to make a checklist of the things they need to do each morning. How might that work?"

Patty pouted, "Mom. It's not like I'm a little kid or something. Gall! It's not like you need to tell me what to do."

"That's a relief!" June nodded, "I guess it would be sad if I had to do that. Anyway, I have a lot to do today, so I'll be leaving for the mall in one hour."

"That's too soon! I haven't even washed my hair yet!"

June remembered to describe what she'd be doing...rather than trying to tell her daughter what to do. With sweetness in her voice, she replied, "I know. I've got a lot to do today, so my car will be leaving in an hour."

As they drove to the mall, June's thoughts wandered. "It's amazing how fast she moved! I didn't have to remind her once. If she can get organized this fast to go to the mall, she's certainly able to get down to the bus stop on time!"

Molasses moves faster on a cold winter day than Patty moved on Monday morning. It was tough. June fought the urge to blab. She kept her mouth shut. She didn't nag, she didn't remind, and she didn't yell when Patty ran back into the house screaming, "Mom! The bus driver didn't even wait!"

With love in her voice, she replied, "Wow. It sounds like you've really got a problem. Beth will be here to drive you to school. You may want to think about how you are going to pay her for her time. I'm leaving. I love you."

June had thought it through. She'd planned it out. As she walked out the door, her best friend arrived on the scene. "Thanks for the favor, Beth. Yes. She missed it! I need to run. I can't wait to hear how she reacts when you ask her how she plans to pay you for driving her to school! I'll call you later."

Did June give her daughter an incredibly valuable gift that morning? With this gift, will Patty be far more successful and happy at work some day? Why?

Bosses are rarely willing to show up at their employees' homes each morning to make sure they get to work on time.

The Fourth "E" of Love and Logic: Experience

There seem to be two types of children. The rarest type is born holding a dove. In the dove's beak is an olive branch. As soon as the umbilical cord is cut, they look up at their parents and say, "Wow! It looks like you guys are sort of stressed. I'm here to help. Just let me know what you need."

These are the rare children who devote their lives to anticipating what we want so that they can do it before we ask. They're careful to extract every bit of wisdom from each and every word we speak. They're slow to make mistakes, because they're quick to learn from our brilliant advice.

There's a far more common and exciting type of child. This type is born smoking a cigar and wearing little red boxing gloves. Before the umbilical cord is cut, they shout, "Before you cut that let's make sure we know who's in charge here! Me! Yeah, and don't you forget it!"

These are the youngsters who motivate their parents to purchase parenting books. As they grow, it seems they devote the lion's share of their attention to figuring out what we want... so that they can do the opposite. They're quick to blow it because they're slow to listen. Instead of gaining wisdom from our words, they gain it from making plenty of mistakes and experiencing their consequences.

The fourth "E" of Love and Logic stands for Experience. Few of us can proudly proclaim that we've learned all of life's most important lessons by carefully listening to others and making great decisions. Most of us have to admit that our road to wisdom has been paved with lots of mistakes. Nothing provides more motivation to make good decisions than the sting associated with experiencing the results of making bad ones.

Nothing provides more motivation to make good decisions than the sting associated with experiencing the results of making bad ones.

Out of tremendous love, many parents steal from their children by making sure that they never make any mistakes...or by rescuing them from the consequences of their mistakes. With the greatest of intentions, June spent the first twelve years of her daughter Patty's life trying to make sure that she never slipped up...

Hurry up. You're going to miss the bus.

Don't forget your lunch money. If you don't eat lunch, you're going to be hungry.

Whatever you do, don't forget your homework. You don't want to get a bad grade.

With each and every one of these lectures and reminders, June robbed her daughter of an opportunity to learn when the price tags were small. She also deprived her of an opportunity to learn skills critical for success in the workplace and in life.

It's true. Mistakes suffer from inflation. Their cost goes up each and every day. Missing the bus and being late to elementary school bears a far smaller price than being late to your job. Forgetting a homework assignment in middle school is clearly more affordable than blowing an important project assigned by your boss. Using bad table manners at age three is cheaper than using them during a lunch meeting at work. Wasting one's allowance at age seven is a bargain compared to mismanaging company funds at age 27. Crashing your tricycle on the lawn is far less costly than crashing the company delivery van on I-95!

Love and Logic parents hope and pray each and every day:

> *Please let my child blow it today…when the price tag is small. If he can make enough small mistakes today, and experience their consequences, maybe, just maybe, he'll develop a voice in his head that constantly asks, "I wonder what the consequences of my next decision will be?" Maybe, just maybe, this'll give him the wisdom to avoid making far more serious mistakes later in life.*

In the past, June had also stolen from her daughter by rescuing her from her poor decisions and bad behavior. It had always been easier to drive her to school when she missed the bus. It had always been more comfortable to do her chores rather than expect her to complete them. It had always been easier to let her off the hook instead of holding her accountable. Thanks to the encouragement she received from Mrs. Apple, she was ready and able to make some big changes. As she drove to work, she smiled at the thought of finally getting there on time. She smiled as she imagined how shocked Patty must have been when Beth arrived and told her that she had to pay her for the taxi trip to school. She grinned as she wondered how Patty was going to pay for the ride, and she felt a little inkling of hope that this new approach might just work a little better than lecturing, threatening, nagging, bribing, and eventually backing down.

The Fifth "E" of Love and Logic: Empathy

Ten-year-old Todd would rather go for a tonsillectomy than do his chores. His parents, Mr. and Mrs. Thomas used to doubt that he could do them without being reminded at least three or four times. That is, until they saw this special show on their public television channel. During the show this grandfatherly old gentleman named Jim Fay talked about this approach called Love and Logic. Best of all, he gave them hope that maybe Todd could really learn to listen the first time.

From this show, they learned some basic steps for getting kids to do their chores without reminders and without pay:

- Don't say, "Do it now." Instead, give your child a deadline, such as, "Just have the trash taken out and the lawn raked by Sunday at 5 PM."
- Use the time this buys you to consider what you are going to do if your child refuses or forgets to do the chore.
- Don't nag or remind. Just hope that they will blow it...so that they can learn from their mistake.
- Let empathy and consequences do the teaching.

While still quite doubtful, Mr. and Mrs. Thomas decided to give it a whirl. "Todd? We could really use your help. Will you please vacuum and dust the living room? Thanks."

"Awe, man!" Todd protested, "I told Roger that I'd go over to his house this morning."

"That's not a problem," they answered. "Just have it done before your bedtime tonight."

As Todd rushed out the door, Mr. and Mrs. Thomas had plenty of time to think. "What will we do if he does a sloppy job, forgets, or simply refuses? How will we muster the self-control required to keep our mouths shut? How will we pull this off so that Todd learns responsibility rather than resentment?"

Let's consider for a moment two different parents responding to the same misbehaving child with the very same consequence. Which one will enjoy the very best results? Which is setting the stage for responsibility? Which is upping the odds for resentment?

Parent "A"

CHILD: "It wasn't my fault! The ball flew up and hit the window."

PARENT: "Oh, so it was the ball's fault. For crying out loud, don't give me that! You were horsing around! That's why it happened. How many times do I have to tell you to be more careful around the house?"

CHILD: "But it…"

PARENT: "Don't give me that! You're going to pay for that window, Mister. I mean it! I tell you and I tell you to be more careful, but you just won't listen. It's about time you learned a little responsibility! You look at me when I'm talking to you! You're paying for that window. I mean it!"

Parent "B"

CHILD: "It wasn't my fault! The ball flew up and hit the window."

PARENT: "Oh no. I bet you feel awful."

CHILD: "But it just flew up there!"

PARENT: "I hate it when that sort of thing happens to me. This is so sad. Give me a hug."

CHILD: "It wasn't my fault."

PARENT: "I know. I love you so much."

CHILD: "Huh?"

PARENT: "This is so sad. How are you planning to pay for that window?"

As this scenario unfolds, which parent has the most angry and resentful child? Which has the most confused one?

Which child is now spending most of his time thinking about how unfair things are? Which is spending most of his time thinking about how unwise it was to play ball so close to the house?

Which parent has the highest blood pressure? Which has the lowest?

Which parent is most likely to end up in the nastiest nursing home? Which is more likely to end up in the nicest?

Parent "B" understands the fifth "E" of Love and Logic: Empathy. He knows that consequences provided with empathy enable kids to learn from their mistakes, whereas consequences provided with anger allow them to blame us for the problem. Consequences with empathy force children to think about their poor decisions, whereas consequences with anger allow them to think mostly about our anger. Empathy allows a child's poor decision to remain the "bad guy" while allowing us to remain the "good guy." Empathy also teaches children to be empathetic with others. Employees who display an attitude of empathy toward customers and coworkers are far more successful than those who don't.

Consequences provided with empathy enable kids to learn from their mistakes, whereas consequences provided with anger allow them to blame us for the problem.

Parent "B" also understands how important it is to provide this empathy before describing the consequence...instead of after. When empathy comes first, it opens the child's mind to learning. When the consequence comes first, the child is usually too upset to hear our empathy. As you consider the following examples, remember that the empathy we provide must be sincere. A loving tone of voice will always achieve superior results over one laced with sarcasm:

This is such a drag. Oh, man. I'd love to take you guys over to the pool, but I don't think I have the energy to referee any more of your battles in the back seat of the car.

How sad. You won't hold my hand in the parking lot. It looks like you'll need to stay in the cart as we shop.

This is no good. Your favorite jeans didn't get washed because they weren't in the hamper. It's never fun when you have to wear something you don't like. I'll be doing wash again in a couple of days.

Oh, no. It sounds like you really had a bad day. I talked to your teacher, and she told me how you kept interrupting her when she was trying to teach. The really sad part about this is that the thirty minutes I spent with her on the phone was the thirty minutes I'd set aside to clean up the dog poop out in the yard. Just have it done by dinner time. Thanks.

Dang...that's got to be upsetting. You dropped your MP3 player and now it won't work. If you want some ideas about how you might earn the money to replace it, just let me know.

This really stinks, but I'm so glad you're okay. The most important thing is that you are safe. Feel free to drive the car again as soon as you've found a way to repair the damage. If you want some ideas, just let me know.

This is so sad. You didn't eat your dinner, and now you're hungry. I guess the good thing is that we're going to have a really good breakfast.

Oh, no. I hate it when I forget to do something really important. Do you have any ideas about how you are going to talk to your teacher about this?

Do you remember Todd, the teen who rushed out the door rather than completing his domestic duties? As he returned from his outing with rambunctious Roger, did he have any idea that his parents were cooking up a little Love and Logic at home? Did he entertain any notion that they'd spent most of the afternoon rehearsing how they might lock in their empathy? Did he have any clue that they were now rock solid ready to hold him accountable if he forgot or refused to do his chores?

Up to this point in his life, not a single neuron in his skull believed that it was important to listen to what his parents asked of him…and not a single neuron believed that they would actually do something if he ignored them. This was about to change.

By Todd's bedtime, Mr. and Mrs. Thomas's tongues were sorer than sore. They'd had to bite them all evening just to keep from nagging and reminding. That tends to make a tongue sore! As a result of their carefully crafted plan, Todd's head hit his pillow before he'd given a single thought to his chores. As the sound of the vacuum cleaner floated into his room, he mused, "Ah, life is good! Mom's doing what she loves…cleaning the living room. Tomorrow, I'll be doing what I love…snowboarding!" It wasn't long before the sounds of the vacuum gave way to wonderful dreams of soaring down the slopes.

Before the sun began to creep over the horizon, Todd was rip-roaring-ready to leave. As the first rays began to peek through his window, he couldn't take it any longer. "Mom, it's getting late! Dad, when are we going to leave?"

There was no response.

"Dad! Dad! Where are you guys? It's time to go! We're going to miss the best snow!"

Desperate, Todd looked in the garage. Finding no one, he checked the bathrooms. Still no parents present. Intensifying his search he burst into their bedroom. Oh the horror! There they were, lying comfortably in their bed. "WE NEED TO GO NOW!" Todd screamed in disbelief.

His mother's voice was barely audible from under the blanket covering her head, "Oh, Todd. This is so sad."

"What are you talking about?" Todd urged, "We need to go!"

Dad locked in another sweet and sleepy dose of empathy, "This is such a drag. Oh, man."

"What are you guys talking about?" Todd was clearly perplexed.

Rolling over in bed, Mom broke the bad news, "Todd, the sad thing is that both your dad and I spent all of our driving time doing your chores last night. We'd love to take you, but all of our time and energy's been used up. Will you shut the door behind you so that we can sleep a bit longer? Thanks."

Todd tried screaming. Each time he did, his parents calmly repeated, "We love you too much to argue."

Todd tried threats. To every one, they calmly replied, "We love you too much to argue."

Todd tried guilt. "We love you too much to argue" was still their response.

Todd even resorted to begging and pleading. You guessed it! "We love you too much to argue" was their firm yet loving response.

Todd's life was never the same. As a result of this and other "training sessions," hope replaced doubt for Mr. and Mrs. Thomas. From this experience they learned that they were doing their son no favors by leading him to believe that life is happy for folks who need to be nagged to complete their work. Bosses want employees who can function without needing their mommies and daddies to follow them around reminding them to do their jobs. With a little Love and Logic Todd is well on his way to being the sort of employee that bosses dream of…an independent, responsible individual.

> **Bosses want employees who can function without needing their mommies and daddies to follow them around reminding them to do their jobs.**

Let's get back to Patty the perpetually tardy pre-teen. In the past, her mother would handle her irresponsible dawdling by nagging, yelling, begging, and bailing her out by driving her to school. Since the winds of Love and Logic change were blowing in this home, too, Patty was about to have a significant learning opportunity. Beth, mom's very best friend, was a Love and Logic natural. "Oh…Patty…It must be so frustrating to miss the bus."

"Yeah," Patty agreed. "It's like the bus driver has such an attitude. He never waits. It's like he's so weird."

"Oh…Patty…it must be horrible to have such a weird bus driver," Beth empathized.

"Yeah, it's like so bogus," Patty proclaimed. "And my mom has been like so weird, too. Do you know what she said this morning?"

"What?" Beth begged.

"Like she said that you were going to charge me to take me to school. Can you believe that?"

Continuing to dollop on the empathy, best friend Beth drove the message home, "Wow, this really is a bummer. Have you given any thought to how you plan to pay the fifteen dollars?"

"What!" Patty screamed. "You can't be for real!"

"How are you planning to pay me?" Beth continued, "If you don't have the cash, you can just pay me with something else… like those cosmetics your mom just bought you."

"This is so lame!" Patty pouted.

In soft agreement, Beth replied, "I know."

"Whatever!" Patty screamed, "I thought you were cool."

"I know," Beth repeated.

Patty tried some guilt, "Everybody hates me!"

Beth wasn't fazed. "It's sad that you feel that way."

"Fine!" Patty cried, "I'll just stay at home. You can't make me go to school!"

Beth was ready for that one. Her own kids had tried that when they were Patty's age. "No problem. I charge $7 an hour for babysitting. Let's see...5 hours times 7 dollars an hour..."

Patty was desperate, "Oh, fine! Take the stupid fifteen dollars. I don't care! I wish I were never born! Nobody understands."

As they pulled in front of Andrew Jackson Middle School, and Patty sneered, "It's like you guys just get off on ruining my life!" as she slammed the car door behind her.

And she was madder than a wet cat that afternoon! (If you've ever given a cat a bath, you know how mad this is!)

"Mom!" Patty yelled, "What's your problem?"

With great love in her voice, she replied, "Oh, Patty, I love you too much to argue."

Patty wasn't ready to give up on the good old guilt trip strategy quite yet. "You don't love me!"

Mom softly replied, "I love you too much to argue."

"Yeah, right!" Patty whined, "None of my friends have to put up with this crap!"

Mom simply repeated, "Patty, I love you too much to argue."

Another skill June learned from Mrs. Apple was the ability to go completely brain dead when Patty tried to argue. In the past, Patty had been able to suck her mother into endless arguments. Mrs. Apple taught her how to put an end to that. "June, every time she tries to argue with you, say to yourself, 'Do not think!' Parents who think too hard about what their arguing kids are saying find it far too hard to stay calm and resist the urge to argue back. Just pick a Love and Logic one-liner, and repeat it over and over in a sweet, loving way."

What did Mrs. Apple mean by a "Love and Logic one-liner"? Listed below are some favorites. Successful parents pick just one or two and use them each and every time their kids try to argue.

- I love you too much to argue.
- I know.
- What did I say?
- What do you think?
- It's sad that you feel that way.
- Probably so.

Is Patty becoming better prepared for life now that she knows that her mother will not be bailing her out of her misdeeds? Is she better prepared for success at work now that she's overcoming her dependency on warnings and reminders? Will she be far happier now that she's discovering that arguing and manipulation don't pay? Great parents realize that their homes represent an internship program for life. As this internship program unfolds, the most fortunate kids learn how to keep a job before they ever get one. Kids who learn that arguing doesn't pay with their parents don't make the unfortunate mistake of trying it with their bosses.

**Kids who learn that arguing doesn't pay
with their parents don't make the unfortunate mistake
of trying it with their bosses.**

CHAPTER TWO

The Perspiration Plan vs. the Las Vegas Plan

Teach your kids to have the best work ethic on earth.

During the winter, it snows in Colorado. Yep! Despite this age old fact, Debbie seems to be surprised any time she finds the white stuff on her car in the morning. What's she to do? The weather's bad. She can't help it if she has to scrape her windows and is late for work. You can't control the weather. She can't help it if the snowplow pushes snow in front of the driveway. It isn't her fault if her driveway gets blocked, and it isn't her fault if she can't get to work on those days. You can't control the weather. Did I say that already? Anyway, it isn't her fault. Besides, she lives five miles from work, and the bus stop is a whole three blocks from her house!

Joan lives in Colorado, too. Every evening before bed, she's glued to the TV, waiting eagerly for the latest forecast. Will there be snow? When it looks likely, she sets her alarm clock for an hour earlier. She also parks her car at the top of her long driveway so that she won't have to shovel so much to get out in the morning. The next day, she wakes up early, does a bit of shoveling, clears her car windows, and drives twenty-two miles into work.

Debbie's boss wonders why Joan can make it to work on time when Debbie can't. Does Joan have supernatural abilities allowing her to control the weather? Not likely. Does her snowplow driver take extra care to avoid pushing more snow in front of her driveway? Nope. While she can't control the weather, she does possess a profound advantage...her belief system.

Joan believes that it's not what happens to you, but how you deal with it. She believes that success comes from lots of hard work and determination...not luck. She even believes that how much you're willing to sweat is more important than how smart you are. Joan lives by the Perspiration Plan. Maybe you're lucky enough to know someone like her...someone whose life is guided by the following:

- Luck isn't as important as hard work and determination.
- The quality of my life is mostly determined by the quality of my decisions and behavior.
- When I make mistakes, I can learn from them and do better next time.
- I have the skills to be successful, regardless of how demanding my boss is.
- It doesn't matter how smart I am, as long as I am willing to work harder and learn more than others around me.
- Waiting to win the lottery is a poor use of time!

Debbie's like a cork in the ocean...a leaf in the wind...a pair of dice rolled on a gambling table. Debbie lives by the Las Vegas Plan. She spends most of her life disgruntled with her poor luck, disappointed with the cards she's been dealt, and dismayed with the unfairness of it all. "Nobody understands. Nobody cuts me a break. It's not my fault" are her most common thoughts. You've probably met someone like Debbie...someone whose life has been misguided by the beliefs listed below:

- Someday my ship will come in!
- How am I supposed to be successful if nobody will give me a break?
- It's somebody else's job to make sure that I'm happy and successful.
- If my boss wasn't such a jerk, I'd be okay.
- How am I supposed to be as successful as all of those other people? I wasn't born with a silver spoon in my mouth, you know.
- Someday when I win the lottery, I'm going to…

What are the consequences of these belief systems? First, let's learn from little George. It wasn't long before people started to notice how bright he was. Everything seemed to come easier to him. He learned to walk and talk earlier than most tykes. He used the potty at a younger age than the kids next door. He even learned to tie his shoes with little or no effort. George's parents proudly thought, "This George of ours is a gem! Life's dealt him a lucky hand, and he's sure to have the world by the tail."

George's luck started running out his very first day of kindergarten. "My teacher's mean!" he told his mother. "She made me stand by the wall at recess."

"George, why did she do that?" Mother prodded.

Bottom lip prominently protruding, he pouted, "She blames me for no reason."

The very next day, George's mother marched into his school and made certain that Mrs. Green never picked on George again. "He's just a little child. Don't you understand how sensitive gifted children are?"

Believe it or not, things didn't get any better for George in the first grade. "She never explains anything," he complained. "She just makes you do a bunch of stuff, but she doesn't even help you."

Dad couldn't believe his ears. "What are the schools coming to these days?" he thought. "Not another incompetent teacher!" The very next day, he marched into the principal's office, demanding that George be placed in another classroom. "He needs a teacher who understands the special needs of very bright children. Don't you understand how gifted he is?"

George got a new teacher. All went well until he came home with a homework assignment on the pilgrims. "This is too much," George complained.

"Let me see," Mom asked as she scanned over the requirements. "George, I don't understand why your teachers give you assignments like this. This is tedious. I'll give her a call tomorrow and make sure that she gives you something more appropriate."

I bet you won't believe it! George's second grade teacher wasn't any good either. She talked too fast.

His third grade teacher was even worse. He talked too slow.

His middle school teachers were "boring."

His high school teachers were simply "incompetent."

As an adult, George's luck grew even worse. The college he went to was a big disappointment, his boss fired him for no reason, and now his ex-wife is always on his "case." It's just not fair!

Some may look at George and think, "Poor George. He's had such a horrible turn of luck. Nothing's worked out for him."

Wiser ones reason, "How sad. In all of their well-intentioned efforts to protect George from the world, his parents led him to believe that all he had to do was wait around for the perfect teacher, perfect college, perfect job, and perfect wife." Those who understand the amazing power of belief systems understand that George's began to disable him very early in his life.

George believes:

*If others were just nicer, fairer, more understanding,
or more competent, I'd be okay. My own actions
have no impact on my life.*

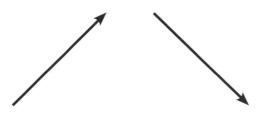

**His original belief
is reinforced:**
*I knew this was going to
happen. Not fair!*

George reasons:
*Why should I exert myself
if my life is really out
of my control?*

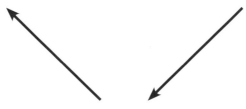

**George just waits around for some better luck
and more understanding people:**
*Why do I always have the worst luck?
Why is everybody always on my case?*

**In all of their well-intentioned efforts to protect George
from the world, his parents led him to believe that
all he had to do was wait around for the perfect teacher,
perfect college, perfect job, and perfect wife.**

Sylvia was born on the same day as George and grew up just down the block. It wasn't long before her parents realized that life was going to be harder for her. It took her longer to learn just about everything. She struggled with walking. She struggled with talking. She was four before she learned to use the potty, and it took endless hours of teaching and practice for her to learn how to tie her shoelaces. Sylvia's parents thought, "Life's going to be a challenge for our lovely little Sylvia. We'll need to teach her how to work harder and longer than any of the other kids."

Sylvia went to the same schools and had the same teachers as George. After her first day of kindergarten, she whined, "My teacher is mean! She made me stand by the wall at recess."

"That's really sad," was her mother's empathetic response.

Bottom lip prominently protruding, Sylvia pouted, "She blames me for no reason."

With a sincere and loving smile, Mother answered, "That must be so hard. If you want some ideas about how to make friends with your teacher, let me know."

Later that evening, Sylvia and her mother talked about how to make friends with teachers. Mom gave her some wise advice: "Sylvia...sweetie...teachers really like it when you look at them when they are talking. And...when they ask you to do something...you do your best to do it. They really like that! Most of all, they love it when kids just work as hard as they can. You've always been good at working longer and harder than other kids."

A week later, Sylvia hugged her mother and said, "My teacher's nice! She lets me play with the computer when I work really hard."

Mom's sage advice also applied to first grade projects about pilgrims. "Mrs. Hornrimm helped me with my project today! She says that she likes to help me because I always do my best."

Mom wasn't surprised. "Oh, Sylvia, I bet it just feels great when your teacher says that! Teachers really like to help kids who always work hard and do their best."

Sylvia's third grade teachers were good, too.

So were her middle school teachers.

Her high school ones were even better.

As an adult, Sylvia enjoys a blessed life. Her boss likes her, her husband loves her, and things just seem to work out well most of the time. She often finds herself wondering, "Why do so many people complain about their bad luck...yet refuse to work hard to change it?"

Some may look at Sylvia and think, "Sylvia's led a charmed life. Everything just seems to go her way. She must have been born with a four leaf clover in her back pocket."

Wiser folks reason, "Sylvia's parents gave her a gift far more valuable than gold, silver, diamonds, or dollars. By preparing her for the world...instead of protecting her from it...they taught her that she has what it takes to control her destiny. By teaching her that hard work and perseverance are more important than luck or intelligence, they gave her the key to success. As a young child, this gift was already shaping the type of life she would have.

Sylvia believes:

If I work long and hard, I can make my life better.

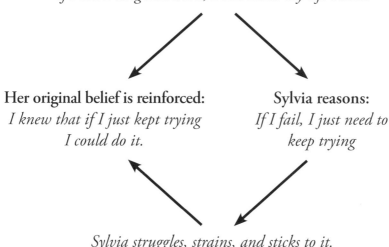

Her original belief is reinforced:
*I knew that if I just kept trying
I could do it.*

Sylvia reasons:
*If I fail, I just need to
keep trying*

Sylvia struggles, strains, and sticks to it.

Each little nugget of success reinforced Sylvia's belief that she's got what it takes to be successful in life. As an adult, she understands that good luck is something that happens when you work your tail off. Unlike George, she spends most of her time feeling fortunate. Also unlike George, she's every employer's dream and wonderful citizen. America desperately needs more people who believe that success comes from hard work rather than handouts.

As we can see from the lives of George and Sylvia, one's belief system, whether they live by the "perspiration plan" or the "Las Vegas plan," has major effects on their...

- motivation to try things that appear difficult
- willingness to keep going when the going gets tough
- personal and professional relationships
- overall achievement
- happiness
- how much fun they are to be around

America desperately needs more people who believe that success comes from hard work rather than handouts.

So, how do we go about raising kids who truly believe that lasting effort is more important than luck? And, what can we do if we have an older child who's slipped into the habit of thinking that it's everybody else's fault she's so unfortunate? In the previous chapter, we learned about the Five "E's" of Love and Logic...and how they apply to teaching basic responsibility and respect. Now let's examine how these very same "E's" can be used to teach our youngsters that the main ingredient of success is sweat.

The First "E" of Love and Logic: Example

Sweat was something that Mr. Hammer knew all about. By shedding lots and lots of it, he'd nailed down a dream position in his company. His salary was super, the benefits were the best, and he got to manage…instead of being managed. There was just one downside to being the big cheese. When anything fell through the cracks, it landed smack dab on his lap. While he loved what he did, all of these little things slipping through cracks left him fairly tuckered-out and stressed by the end of each day. Fortunately for Mr. Hammer he went home to a wonderful wife and son each and every evening. And, each and every evening the conversation was just about the same:

"Hi, honey," Mrs. Hammer would smile as she hugged her hard working husband. "How was your day?"

"Ah…tiring," he'd reply with a frown. "I'll never understand how so many problems can pile up in one day."

"What happened?" she'd inquire.

He'd answer, "Oh…just the same old hassles…but let's not ruin the evening with all of that. It's just great to be home with you guys!"

Little Max, like most little boys, studied his father's every move. No gesture or word passed unnoticed by his curious eyes and ears. By the time he'd entered elementary school, Max was the spitting image of his daddy, Mr. Hammer. That is, with just one exception. Max was a major underachiever, and he spent most of his time complaining about how unfair his teachers were!

With the hard working example set by his parents, how was it that Max managed to acquire such an avoidance of academics? Why was he repulsed by reading and upset by arithmetic? How had he adopted the view that it was someone else's job to make him successful? Why was he living by the "Las Vegas plan" while his parents were clear "Perspiration plan" sorts of folks? His parents were puzzled, and his teachers were perplexed. In desperation, they turned to Ms. Binet, the school psychologist.

She had her hands full, too. Max mastered her IQ tests, clearly showing that he had what it takes to do exceptionally well in school. He showed no signs of the sorts of emotional problems that can interfere with kids performing well in the classroom. There were just no clues…until she asked Max a few simple questions.

"Max, I'm curious. How do you think your parents feel about learning and getting a good education?"

"Uh," he answered, "they think it's really important."

Scratching her head, Ms. Binet probed, "Oh, so they think you should get a good education?"

"Yeah, they want me to be like them," Max agreed.

"Is there something wrong with being like them?" she inquired.

Max appeared just a bit nervous as he stuttered, "Well…no…but…uh."

Ms. Binet was starting to get somewhere, "It sounds like you think there's something wrong with being like your parents."

"It's just that my dad is always tired and stressed out," Max admitted. "He's always saying, 'Get a good education,' but he has one and he's always unhappy."

There it was! That was the missing piece of the puzzle! By the time Max was ten years old, he'd overheard his father venting about work-related frustrations literally thousands of times. Long before then he'd made the following connection:

My dad had to work really hard and learn a lot to be so unhappy. If hard work leads to such hardship, count me out!

Over the past three decades, we've met many kids like Max. From them, we've learned that a sure-fire way to ensure that our children dislike learning is to let them consistently overhear us venting our frustrations about work. When this occurs, kids come to believe that it's far better to wait around for good luck than to risk being miserable by working too hard and getting a good education. From these youngsters, we've also learned that it's never too late to start repairing the damage! If we can switch things around...and make a concerted effort to talk with excitement about our work...it's highly likely that their attitudes about effort will improve.

The First "E" of Love and Logic, Example, gains its power from two types of modeling. The first type, how we act in front of our kids, is obvious. Just about everybody understands that kids copy what they see us doing. From the example set by his mother and father, young Max learned that big people work hard.

The second type of modeling, what our kids overhear us saying, is far less obvious yet arguably more powerful. From the example set when his father repeatedly vented about work, young Max learned that being a big person who works hard is certainly something to be avoided for as long as possible.

There's no strategy more powerful for teaching values than setting a good example by talking about these values within earshot of our kids. If we want our kids to value honesty, we ought to talk about our honesty when their little ears can overhear. If we want them to value self-control, we should do the same. If we want them to value learning and hard work, they'd better overhear us talking about how much happier our own lives are when we learn and work hard. While kids' ears tend to shrink when we lecture, they swell when they overhear us talking about something with great passion.

There's no strategy more powerful for teaching values than setting a good example by talking about these values within earshot of our kids.

Mr. Hammer felt horrible. "It all makes sense to me now! Why didn't I think about that earlier? If I'd just been more careful about the sorts of things I was saying in front of Max, then we wouldn't be in this fix."

Ms. Binet gave him some wise advice. "Beating yourself up about this isn't going to make Max a harder worker. But I have an idea. Let's see what happens if you and his mom start talking with excitement about your learning and hard work."

"Do you think there's hope?" Mr. Hammer asked.

"You bet!" Ms. Binet assured. "I've seen it work with other kids, and I'm pretty sure it'll work with Max. Just make it a goal to let him overhear you saying at least one positive thing about your work each week."

"What else can we do?" Mrs. Hammer pleaded.

Ms. Binet paused, scratched her head, and replied, "If he overhears you saying positive things about his teachers that should help a bit, too."

The Hammers walked out of Ms. Binet's office with a handful of hope and a plan. The sky seemed bluer and the birds sang sweeter. That's until Mr. Hammer realized how hard old habits die. The very next evening, his sweet wife greeted him with a smile and asked, "Hi honey. How'd your day go?"

Before his mind caught up with his tongue, it slipped out of his mouth, "Ah...what a hassle. Jacobson in shipping sent a whole order of..."

It was too late. The words floated in the air like the scent of rotten eggs on a hot summer day. And there was little Max, soaking in every bit of their aroma.

Despite the best of intentions, the very next evening wasn't much better. "Honey, the phone's for you. It's work."

Boom! Faster than a speeding bullet, "Awe for crying out loud. What now?" shot right out of daddy Hammer's mouth. Again, it was too late. Across the table sat little Max the sponge, soaking up each and every word.

There's no tougher job than being a conscientious parent. At times, we feel at a complete loss for what to do. Other times we know what to do yet "forget" to do it because we're tired, stressed, or angry. Still other times, old parenting habits learned early in our lives…from our own parents…get in the way of doing what we know is right. Through years of repetition, these reactions become so automatic that they slip out our mouths with little or no conscious thought. If when we were little, we consistently saw our parents get angry and yell, it's quite likely that we'll be prone to getting angry and yelling. If when we were small, we observed Mom or Dad consistently complaining about each other, we'll be more likely to do the same. If when we were young, we consistently heard our parents complain about their work, it's likely that we'll simply follow suit.

But it's not all gloom and doom for Mr. Hammer! If our kids consistently see us learning from our mistakes and growing, they'll be likely to do the same. A bit discouraged yet even more determined, Mr. Hammer tacked a note right under his son's picture at work. From time to time he'd gaze at Max's smiling face. Then he'd read the note:

I don't need you to be perfect…I just need you to be positive.

Taped inside his briefcase was another copy…right next to a wallet sized picture of Max:

I don't need you to be perfect…I just need you to be positive.

On the dashboard of his car, right under "Unleaded Fuel Only" was yet another:

I don't need you to be perfect…I just need you to be positive.

On his nightstand, next to Max's school picture was one more:

I don't need you to be perfect...I just need you to be positive.

Each night Mr. Hammer dozed off to dreamland imagining Max's marvelous mug and thinking, "He doesn't need me to be perfect...he just needs me to be positive."

A wonderfully strange thing started happening in the Hammer household. When Pop popped through the door each evening after work, the words that squirted out of his mouth started becoming positive instead of pessimistic. A clear sign that things were getting better was when young Max, rather irritated by his father's new-found perkiness, questioned, "What are you so happy about?"

At this precise moment a precious opportunity arose, "Max," he answered, "I just feel great when I've worked hard and I've done my best!"

The Second "E" of Love and Logic: Expectation

If Mr. Hammer had worn dentures, they'd have dropped right out of his mouth and crash-landed on his desk. He'd never seen or heard something so strange in his life. All he could do was sit there stupefied...with his mouth so far open you could drive a truck into it. On the other side of his desk sat Pete's caring mother, busily describing all the reasons why her son was the best candidate for the new position in marketing.

"As I'm sure you've seen, Pete is a real hard worker." She beamed, "You've noticed that, I'm sure. And he's so intelligent. Do you know that his sixth grade science fair project won first prize? He was always far brighter than the other kids his age. And, I'm sure you've also seen how creative he is...haven't you?"

Mr. Hammer pinched himself multiple times. It hurt. "When it hurts," he thought, "that means you aren't dreaming." And since he wasn't asleep, that meant that there really was an employee's PARENT sitting across the desk from him, attempting to negotiate a promotion for her son! After recovering a bit from the shock…and all the pinching…some not-so-sweet thoughts began to bounce around in his head. "She's got to be kidding! I couldn't care less about some stupid volcano he made in the sixth grade. She has no idea how close that kid of hers is to being canned. Now it makes sense why he thinks that it's everybody else's job to do his work!"

While the names have been changed to protect the guilty, THIS REALLY DOES HAPPEN! Over the past two decades employers and college professors are seeing more and more parents walk into their offices demanding that their adult children be given better pay, better grades, nicer offices, more second chances, etc. I didn't believe it at first. I thought, "No way! This cannot be!" After it happened to me…in my own business…I realized that never before in history have there been more parents so deeply dedicated to rescuing their kids from the real world. I, like most bosses, am not impressed when parents show up at work to advocate for their adult children.

As he drove home, Mr. Hammer found himself hammering the throttle a bit too hard. He just couldn't wait to get home and tell his wife what happened today at work. Then a thought popped up, causing his right foot to lighten. "Max needs me to be positive. I'd better not share this when he can hear." Almost home, more thoughts jumped into his head. "Just the other day, you and Max's mom drove to the school and demanded that his teacher give him less homework. The day before, you told his coach that he deserved to start instead of being second string. For three days in row, his mom has driven to his school to give him his forgotten lunch money, homework, and field trip permission slip. This morning, you told him that you'd call his coach and make sure that he was starting the next game."

Bosses are not impressed when parents show up at work to advocate for their adult children.

Suddenly Mr. Hammer's right foot was barely weighty enough to get him home. "Maybe," he mused, "we aren't that different from Pete's parents."

Most over-protective parents aren't nearly as extreme as Pete's... or Max's. Nevertheless, they do a great deal of damage over the years by slowly eroding their children's sense of personal responsibility and self-worth. Each time they rescue their kids from the consequences of their decisions, they make it just a bit harder for them to mature into happy and productive members of the workforce...and society. Every time they try to create an easier world for their kids by trying to make other adults bend the rules or lower their expectations, they rob their kids of responsibility and self-respect.

The second "E" of Love and Logic stands for Expectation. In the previous chapter, we drove home the point that kids live up to...or down to...the expectations we send. When we try to prepare the world for our kids, instead of preparing them for the world, we send the following messages:

- You can't cope with this world, so I'll make sure that all goes smoothly.
- You shouldn't have to work too hard. I'll make sure that people don't expect too much from you.
- You have no control over your own life. You need others to make sure that you're successful.

Nobody sets out to send such sad messages. It's safe to say that very few parents make a written plan for teaching their kids to rely on luck and handouts instead of perspiration and perseverance. What typically happens instead is that we get started with the best of intentions, fall into the habit of trying too hard to make things perfect for our children, and wake up one day realizing that our kids have become a bit "responsibility challenged."

Every time we try to create an easier world for our kids by attempting to make other adults bend the rules or lower their expectations, we rob them of responsibility and self-respect.

There's great hope! If you're reading these pages and thinking, "Aw, man, he's talking about me! If I'd only…" don't despair. There's no such thing as a perfect parent. Imperfect ones have been raising great kids since the dawn of creation. We're all in this together, learning as we go. By the time you finish this chapter, you'll have learned some time-tested techniques for showing your kids that they've got what it takes to solve their own problems and experience success. As you apply these techniques, you'll also learn that you've got what it takes to experience a lot more fun with your kids!

The Third "E" of Love and Logic: Education

Max was hotter than a jalapeño! "It's not fair! You told me that you were going to call Coach and tell him to start me!"

His father replied, "I know. But then I started worrying about how much your mom and I have stolen from you."

"Huh?" Max inquired with confusion. "What are you talking about?"

Dad continued, "Well…Max…we've been stealing learning opportunities."

"Huh?"

Mr. Hammer continued, "We've been solving all of your problems...and robbing you of opportunities to learn that you have what it takes to solve them yourself."

"That's stupid," Max complained. "When are you calling Coach? The game is in two days."

Dad remembered something he'd learned from Love and Logic. When a kid wants to argue, just keep repeating the same statement in a caring tone of voice. "Max...I love you too much to argue."

"I'm not arguing, Dad. When are you going to call?"

"I love you too...

Max interrupted, "You don't love me!"

This time it was hard, but Dad managed to stay on track. "Max...I love you too much to argue. I will listen when your voice is calm like mine."

Before slamming his bedroom door behind him, Max managed to sling just one more verbal arrow, "My friends have parents that love them!"

The third "E" of Love and Logic stands for Education. We all understand that kids need our instruction and guidance to develop essential life skills. The problem arises when we go about doing this and crash into a brick wall of arguing, ignoring, or eye-rolling. How would Max react if his father marched right into his room and made an elaborately eloquent speech about the importance of learning problem-solving skills? What are the chances that Max would look his father in the eye and announce, "Dad...up until this point I thought you were completely off base. But after you put it that way, it really makes sense. Now I can see that you have my best interests in mind. There are going to be some big changes around here with my behavior."

Parents who understand Love and Logic understand that it's never productive to reason with a drunk...or a child who's drunk on emotion. Instead, the chances of success are far higher when we save our talks for times when our kids are calm and we are calm. Parents well-versed in Love and Logic also know that children are far more likely to learn from our wise words if we apply the following steps for guiding them to own and solve their problems:

Step one: Provide a strong and sincere dose of empathy.
As we've already seen, empathy opens the heart and the mind to learning. There's an old yet wise cliché that reminds the following:

Nobody really cares how much we know until they know how much we care.

Yep! Folks are far more likely to open their ears to us when we've first opened ours to them. This means that we've taken the time to put ourselves in their shoes by listening and trying our best to understand. This also means that we've resisted the urge to jump right in with our two cents' worth.

It's also critical to remember that most of the communication taking place between two people is nonverbal. The tone of our voice, our facial expression, and our general posture can either support the empathetic words coming out of our mouth…or completely cancel them out.

Step two: Ask, "What do you think you are going to do?"
This simple question sends a very powerful and positive expectation regarding their ability to solve the challenges they encounter. It also clarifies that the problem is theirs to solve, rather than ours.

Step three: When the child says, "I don't know," ask, "Would you like to hear some ideas?"
If your child shrugs her shoulders and mumbles, "I don't know" when you ask, "What do you think you are going to do?" it

means that they're like the vast majority of youngsters on the planet. It's the rare child, indeed, who responds with a wonderfully wise list of options for solving their problem. That's why we move on to step three by asking, "Would you like to hear some ideas?"

Why's it so important to ask this question…rather than simply telling our kids what they might do? As a general rule, people are far more likely to listen to our ideas when they know they don't have to. You don't need to be Sigmund Freud to know that control is a major drive for most of us. When we share control by first asking permission to provide our thoughts, our kids are far less likely to hoard control by closing their ears and minds.

When we empathize, listen, and ask permission before spouting off, most kids are willing to hear our thoughts. While this is typically the case, what's a parent do when their child and stubbornly replies, "No"? Wise parents sidestep the power-struggle by calmly responding, "Thanks for being honest with me. If you change your mind, I'll be happy to share my ideas."

At this point in the discussion, many parents ask, "What do I do if my child refuses to solve the problem?" Two options exist. The first involves simply allowing your child to live with the natural consequences of having a problem that isn't solved. This option applies when the problem only affects your child and the natural consequences would provide a great learning experience for your child. The second option involves giving your child a deadline for solving the problem…and being willing to step in if your child fails to meet this deadline. This option applies when the problem affects others or the natural consequences of failing to solve it are too great. A parent applying this second option might say, "This problem really does need to be solved. If it isn't taken care of by tomorrow evening at six, I'll have to do something about it."

If the child doesn't solve the problem, then it's time for the parent to solve the problem…and provide some sort of consequence that leaves the child thinking, "Oh, man. It would have been a lot easier for me to take care of this than to let my mom handle it!" Yes! Smart parents always make sure that the consequence for refusing to solve a problem results in far greater effort and inconvenience for their child than simply solving the problem in the first place.

Step four: Give your child just two or three options and ask, "How will that work for you?" after each.

When we're sharing options for solving the problem, children always respond better to, "Some kids decide to…" rather than "You should…" Again, we're talking about the power of control. "Some kids decide to…" communicates an element of choice. It's easy to see how "You should…" doesn't.

Parents often worry that they won't have any good ideas at this point. When this happens say, "I just realized that I don't have any good ideas right now. Let's talk about this later…after I've had a chance to think a bit more. Maybe you'll have some good ideas by then, too."

Kids often come up with great ideas when we fall back on this stall technique. That's why it's never the end of the world if you find yourself momentarily stumped. When parents become dumb, it often forces their kids to become a lot smarter! People who understand this irony also know the benefit of giving a lousy option for solving the problem first. Since kids tend to reject the first suggestion we give, this allows us to avoid wasting a good one. More importantly it forces our kids to think a bit harder as we help them evaluate the possible consequences of each option.

> **When parents become dumb, it often forces their kids to become a lot smarter.**

People who go through life frequently asking themselves, "How might this action I'm about to take work out?" lead far happier lives than those who don't. Wouldn't it be great if there were some way that we could teach our kids to do this? Wouldn't it be great if we could coach them along so that they eventually had a little voice inside their heads that constantly evaluated the consequences of their actions...before they actually performed them? Asking, "How will this work for you?" after providing options for solving the problem does exactly that!

Step five: Resist the urge to tell your child which solution to use. For many parents, this is the hardest part. As they discuss options for solving the problem, a favorite pops out at them. They reason, "If my child would just pick this one, then all will be right with the world." Acting on the urge to tell our kids which solution to apply almost always backfires. If they do what we tell them, and it goes poorly, we're the bad guy...and no learning takes place. If they do what we tell them and it goes well, we've stolen the opportunity for them to look at themselves with pride and say, "I chose that one! I did it!"

Parents who understand Love and Logic keep responsibility for solving the problem squarely on their child's shoulders by saying, "I know that you have what it takes to make a good decision on this. Good luck. Let me know how this works out for you."

Because we don't apply this process for life and death problems, it's never the end of the world if our kids pick crumby solutions and blow it. In fact, with every mistake they make, they grow and learn. It's true. The road to wisdom is paved with mistakes...and the consequences associated with making them.

The chances of success are far higher when we save our talks for times when our kids are calm and we are calm.

The very next evening, Mr. Hammer decided to give these five steps a try. Starting with step one, he locked in a strong dose of empathy. "Max, it's pretty clear that getting a starting position on the team is really important to you. It must be so frustrating to sit on the bench and see the other kids playing."

Max agreed, "Yeah...Dad...have you called the coach yet?"

Deciding to ignore the fact that Max had already asked that question about 100 times, he moved on to step two, "What do you think you could do to make Coach consider giving you a shot?"

Shrugging his shoulders, Max mumbled, "I don't know."

Dad went to step three, "Would you like some ideas?"

"Uh, I guess so."

Now it was time for step four. Just like a Love and Logic pro, Dad started with an option that Max was sure to dislike. "Some kids change their minds and decide that starting isn't that important to them. How would that work for you?"

Max was shocked! "What? That won't work. I HAVE to start!"

"Well, Max, some kids decide to show the coach that they're willing to work harder than the other kids on the team. How would that work for you?"

"I already work hard. He just doesn't see me doing it."

"Max, I only have one other idea. Some kids decide to talk to the coach and ask him to describe what they need to work on so that they have a chance at starting. How would that work for you?"

"Dad, why won't you just call him? It'll only take a couple minutes."

Remembering step five, Dad patted Max on the shoulder, smiled, and said, "Good luck. Your mom and I will love you regardless of how this turns out."

Stomping off to his room, Max uttered under his breath, "It's like I have to do everything around here."

Mr. Hammer discovered one of parenting's greatest ironies: When we do the right thing with challenging kids, it often looks and feels like the wrong thing in the short term. It's not easy expecting our kids to own and solve their own problems. It often leaves us feeling like we haven't done enough to help. The good feelings come later, when we begin to see how much happier and more responsible they're becoming.

The Fourth "E" of Love and Logic: Experience

A slight burning odor permeated the Hammer household as Max paced a bare spot into his bedroom carpet. Back and forth he went, smoke coming from each of his ears. For the first time in his young life, Max was thinking long and hard about one of his problems. What a lucky kid! There's no better preparation for successful adulthood than lots of practice thinking during one's childhood.

There's no better preparation for successful adulthood than lots of practice thinking during one's childhood.

Mr. and Mrs. Hammer were also hard at thought, trying to keep themselves from rushing in and rescuing him from his dilemma. The hardest part of guiding our kids to own and solve their problems is the final step…allowing them to take responsibility for the final solution while keeping our mouths shut. The fourth "E" of Love and Logic stands for Experience. Do our children get any experience owning and solving their problems if we don't also allow them to experience the good…or not-so-good… consequences associated with the solutions they choose?

"I'm quitting the team!" Max mouthed to his mother.

"Oh, honey, what happened?" she inquired.

Max steamed, "Coach said that I needed to work on my attitude and show that I am a team player."

Trying her best not to jump into his problem, Mom let go with a nice little bit of empathy. "It sounds like you are so upset. I bet that was hard to hear."

"Well, what are you going to do?" Max demanded. "You need to call him and tell him that he can't talk to me that way!"

"Max," she answered with great love in her voice, "Your dad and I have decided that this is a problem that you'll need to solve. Would you like some ideas?"

Flailing himself toward his bedroom, he protested, "Awe… man! Not that stuff again!"

Did I already say that it's not easy being a great parent? Mom was finding this out first hand! When we give our children the gift of owning some of their problems, sometimes they are going to be disappointed or upset. That's why smart parents only use these techniques when they're sure that they can stick to the plan, even when they feel horrible down deep.

There will also be gloriously glad times when we allow our kids to tackle problems and things go great! How we respond when our kids succeed is just as important as how we react when they don't. For years and years, parents and educators were told that it was critical to praise kids anytime they did something well. Some of us were even taught to behave a bit like cheerleaders, constantly saying things like, "That's great!" Wow!" "You are so smart!" or "Super!"

There's nothing wrong with occasional, spontaneous praise. There are times when we all see kids doing great things and just find "That's great!" slipping right out of our mouths. In contrast, when we barrage children with praise, we often see some very unfortunate results. Over the past three decades, employers have seen increasing numbers of individuals who believe that they can't make it through the day unless somebody tells them how bright, special or wonderful they are. They also appear to believe that they shouldn't have to work unless they get a continuous helping of such feedback. Last time I checked, few bosses are really keen on spending all day jumping up and down with pom-poms.

Last time I checked, few bosses are really keen on spending all day jumping up and down with pom-poms.

There's been another unintended and very sad consequence of the "praise movement"...more and more people who believe that intelligence is more important than hard work and perseverance. When children are constantly told how smart they are, they come to believe that smartness is the key to success. When they run into tough tasks that don't leave them feeling so smart, they're quick to give up and say, "It's too hard" or "I'm dumb." Do you know someone who'll only keep trying if they know for sure that they can be successful with little or no effort?

Love and Logic offers a powerful technique for helping children understand that success is more a function of strains than brains. When children come to believe this, they are far more willing to keep trying even when things get hard. Experiment with the following steps:

Step one: Post the following three statements prominently in your home.

- *I worked hard.*
- *I kept trying.*
- *I've been practicing.*

As we learned early in this chapter, high achievers attribute their success...or lack of it...to factors within their control. They live by the "perspiration plan." In contrast, low achievers live by the "Las Vegas plan." That is, they attribute the outcomes of their actions to factors completely beyond their control. Obviously, each of the statements above represents a high achiever attribution.

Step two: When your child succeeds with something, describe to them what they did...without praising. Then ask, "How did you do that?"
Instead of saying, "That's great," "Wow," or "Awesome," be as specific as possible. Here are some examples:

- *I noticed that you got number nine on your math worksheet correct. How did you do that?*
- *The "T" you wrote in cursive looks just like the example your teacher wrote for you. How did you do that?*
- *You sat in the restaurant the whole time without fighting with your brother. How did you do that?*
- *You took out the trash and cleaned your bathroom mirror without being asked. How did you do that?*
- *You fixed your bike without help. How did you do that?*

Step three: If your child says, "I don't know," provide the three possibilities listed under step one.
The entire sequence might sound something like:

Parent: "Your piano teacher told me that you learned all of your scales. How did you do that?"

Child: "I don't know."

Parent: "Well, either you worked hard, kept trying, or practiced. Which one do you think?"

Child: "Um, I don't know."

Parent: "If you did know which one it was, which one would it be?"

Child: "Uh, I guess I practiced."

Parent: "I guess so!"

Many people ask, "Why can't I just tell my child why they were successful. Wouldn't that be a whole lot easier?"

A powerful principle of human attitude change goes as follows:

What you say to me is your reality. What I say to myself will become mine.

Here's the key: Get your child to say either "I worked hard," "I kept trying," or "I've been practicing" as often as possible. The more frequently one of these rolls off of their own tongue, the more likely they will truly come to believe that hard work and perseverance is far more important than luck or handouts.

When children are constantly told how smart they are, they come to believe that smartness is the key to success. When they run into tough tasks that don't leave them feeling so bright, they're quick to give up and say, "It's too hard" or "I'm dumb."

Three weeks later, Max was still on the team and excited beyond excited, "Coach says that I get to start next week if I keep a good attitude!"

Using his new skills, Mr. Hammer replied, "He's seeing some big changes in you. Why do you think that's the case?"

"Uh, I don't know. I guess 'cause I got a better attitude."

"How did you do that?" Mother asked. "Do you think it's because you've been working hard, you decided to keep trying, or you've been practicing?"

Max paused, "I guess it's because I kept trying."

Patting Max on the back, Dad replied, "I bet that feels great."

Max is indeed a lucky boy! Let's review:

- By overhearing the positive **Example** of his father talking with excitement about his job, he's learning that maybe… just maybe…hard work leads to happiness instead of hardship.
- Because his parents are now sending the **Expectation** that he's capable of living with the consequences of his decisions, he's learning that he's the one who's responsible for determining the course of his life.
- By guiding him to own and solve his problems, they're giving him a valuable **Education** about how to tackle the troubles he encounters.
- By allowing him to **Experience** the consequences of his decisions, he's seeing that good decisions lead to far happier outcomes than poor ones.
- Through all of this, Max is beginning to understand that hard work and determination are far more important than luck, intelligence, or handouts.

The Fifth "E" of Love and Logic: Empathy

When he was very small, Mike soon came to believe that he messed up far more often than any other kid on the planet. He believed that he spilled more milk, got in more trouble on the playground, lost more homework assignments, and spent more time in the principal's office. When Mike messed up, Mike's mother made sure he knew how angry she was...

"Mike! You spilled your milk! How many times do I have to tell you to be more careful? You get a towel and clean that up right now!"

"Mike! Didn't I tell you to take out the trash? I am so sick and tired of having to remind you."

Mike knew that he was really in trouble when she used his full legal name...

"Michael Mumfrey Mumford! You are in big trouble, Mister! I got another call from the school. You just earned yourself some extra chores!"

It wasn't long before Mike lost something even more impor-tant than his homework assignments...his hope. "Why try?" he thought. "I can't do anything right. I'm stupid."

Along the way, Mike's well-meaning yet massively stressed mother learned about Love and Logic from her best friend. "It's a way of parenting that makes it a lot easier and more fun," claimed her buddy. "I'm taking a Love and Logic class at the school. You should come along."

With a reluctant sense of obligation, Mike's mother dragged herself to the class. There she sat, wondering how she was going to make it through two hours of psychological mumbo-jumbo. The instructor popped in a video by this guy named Dr. Charles Fay. As she watched, she started to giggle. The stories on the video were actually funny! And the ideas seemed to make sense, too! Then a twinge of sadness touched her heart as she began to think about her own mother. She remembered how angry her mother used to get when she misbehaved. She remembered how resentful and hopeless all of that anger left her. Then she suddenly realized something that made her shudder. She was parenting just like her mother!

From the video, she learned that consequences provided with anger result in resentment. She also learned that the best way to make sure that a child doesn't learn from a consequence is to get really mad and say, "I hope you learned your lesson!" Possibly the saddest thing she learned was that children who associate mistakes with anger quickly learn to avoid doing anything remotely challenging...anything that might result in them making a mistake. "Maybe," she wondered, "that's why Mike always forgets to do what I say."

Children who associate mistakes with anger quickly learn to avoid doing anything remotely challenging.

Mike's mother felt about two inches tall. That is, until she heard in the video that it's never too late to turn things around. Her ears perked up. Then she heard Dr. Fay describing how to replace anger with empathy by memorizing just one small empathetic statement. On the palm of her left hand she wrote, "This is so sad." This was the one she'd use. All she had to do was glance at that hand and remind herself, "sadness instead of anger...sadness instead of anger...sadness instead of anger."

Many of us were raised by well-meaning parents who believed that they had to show plenty of anger so that we'd learn from our mistakes. While most of us probably turned out just fine anyway, we find it very difficult to apply more positive and effective techniques with our kids. It's like our parents from childhood reside somewhere inside of our skulls. These "internal parents" remain silent until our kids start to act up or make mistakes. Then they awaken and start shouting, "Show 'em how mad you are! Give 'em what-for! For crying out loud, let 'em have it!"

The fifth "E" of Love and Logic stands for Empathy. The first step in making the transition from parenting with anger to parenting with empathy involves memorizing just one simple empathetic statement. Listed below are some favorites. Remember:

How we say these is just as important as what we say! It's critical that our tone of voice and body language also convey empathy… rather than sarcasm or anger.

- *This is so sad.*
- *Oh…that's never good.*
- *How sad.*
- *What a bummer.*
- *This stinks.*
- *Dang.*
- *Oh, man.*

Mike's mother knew that overriding her old habits wasn't going to be easy. That's why she used up an entire pad of yellow sticky notes. On each page she wrote, "This is so sad." Then she plastered them all over the house…on her alarm clock, on the bathroom mirror, on the inside of her toilet seat, on the refrigerator. … Everywhere she looked, she saw, "This is so sad."

The second step in learning to replace anger with empathy is allowing yourself to keep it simple by using this single empathetic statement each and every time your child makes a poor decision. After spending a week seeing "This is so sad" everywhere she looked, Mike's mother was ready to go for it. The very next afternoon, Mike got off the school bus braced for a verbal bruising. Sure, he'd thrown cheese on the ceiling of the cafeteria, but it wasn't really his fault. Corey made him do it.

As he walked in the door, his mother met him with a hug. "Hey, guy, how was your day?"

A bit confused, he thought, "Maybe there's hope. Maybe the principal forgot to call. Maybe she'll just forget…forever."

Then he muttered, "Uh, good?"

"This is so sad," Mom replied in the saddest yet sweetest

tone she could muster, "I spent twenty minutes talking to your teacher about what happened at lunch."

"Yeah but it wasn't my fault. Corey—"

With a loving hug, she continued, "The saddest part is that I was planning to use that time to clean up the dog poop out in the yard. Just get that done by the end of the day. Thanks!"

Mike suddenly became too confused to speak. What had his mother been smoking?

Mike's mother felt ten feet tall! As she watched her son wander around the yard with a shovel and a plastic bag, she thought, "Maybe there's hope for both of us!"

CHAPTER THREE

Is That Rain…
or Liquid Sunshine?

Help your kids learn to love work rather than loathe it.

Weather Alert! Weather Alert! This is not a test! Doppler radar predicts a 95% chance of severe winds, dark clouds, and rain over Ms. Jones' cubicle. Be advised! This weather system is moving at the speed of sound toward surrounding office space. Stormie Weathers, Channel 9 meteorologist, suggests taking cover by plastering Post-It notes over your ears, humming, and hunkering under your desk.

It's sad but true. Ms. Jones sees everything through mud-colored glasses. Life is just one big pain after another, and all of these big pains come oozing out whenever the boss is out of sight. "These people are so stupid! They call and want product like yesterday. Who do they think they are? And then they get all huffy. It's like they think that we can just drop everything and send it out now. And then it takes them forever to find their credit card. Like, why don't they have it right in front of them when they call?"

But there's more.

"Did you see Keri talking to Mr. Cheddar yesterday? She is such a kiss-up! And he falls for it! Mark my words. She'll be getting a raise. How lame. And I heard that her husband left her. No wonder. I mean, who could put up with that? She tries that phony stuff with me, but I know it's all just a big act."

And there's even more!

"Cheddar calls this a bonus? What a joke! With all the dough they're raking in around here, that's all they can do? And he's so clueless. These new procedures are totally bogus. It just shows that brains aren't what it takes to get to the top around here."

Mr. Cheddar, Ms. Jones' boss, is struggling to get a handle on why the office isn't the warm, friendly, and productive place it used to be. He wonders, "Why is there so much bickering going on? Why does it seem like everything is moving at a snail's pace? Why does tension hang in the air like the smell of a skunk farm during an earthquake?"

It takes him a while to figure it out, but the clues start rolling in. Tugging at his beard, he ponders, "Things started going sour just about the time I hired Ms. Jones. Hmm? Every time there's an office spat, she seems to be involved. Hmm? And she's the one that seems to get all of the irate customer calls. I wonder if those customers were irate before she answered the phone... or just after? Hmm? And, to be honest, the week she was out with the flu felt like the first warm day of spring. Ms. Jones has got to go!"

Mr. Cheddar knows that there's nothing more damaging to a business than a chronically negative employee. He knows something else...just one of them can bring down an entire team. Like a tiny virus, their negativity infects and spreads, eventually killing the spirit of the group. Regardless of how much he likes Ms. Jones, he's forced to let her go before the weather gets any worse.

There's nothing more damaging to a business than a chronically negative employee… and there's nothing more damaging to a nation than a chronically negative populace.

Ms. Smith sees life through rose-colored glasses. Where Ms. Jones sees rain, she sees liquid sunshine. The same bonus perceived by Ms. Jones is seen by Ms. Smith as a big blessing. What's viewed as a huge hassle to Ms. Jones is heralded as a challenge by Ms. Smith. Although she never intends to, Ms. Smith is the type of employee that really irritates Ms. Jones. Why? Because she's far too perky! She's even nice in the mornings…before she has coffee! "How incredibly annoying!" thinks Ms. Jones. "Where does she get off being so happy all of the time? If I had an easy life like hers, I'd be all smiles, too."

Mr. Cheddar knows that optimistic employees are more valuable than gold. When problems arise, they help the group see opportunities for improvement…instead of insurmountable obstacles. Through their positive, "take the high road" attitude, they model teamwork, making it difficult for negative employees to sour the soup by moaning and complaining behind the boss's back. From the positive energy buzzing around them the entire team gains momentum. "The only problem with the Ms. Smiths of the world," laughs Mr. Cheddar, "is that other companies see how good they are and try to steal them from you!"

Wise employers understand that optimistic employees are more valuable than gold. From the positive energy buzzing around them the entire team gains momentum.

Why is Ms. Smith so much happier and more positive than Ms. Jones? Does she have a nicer car, a bigger house, a larger bank account, or a better position at work? Does her optimism spring from her life circumstances or from how she thinks about her life circumstances? While it's far easier to stay upbeat when life's serving roses rather than rotten eggs, the most dazzling difference between positive and negative people has more to do with their thinking than how much life is stinking.

In the previous chapter we learned about two different approaches to life: the Perspiration Plan and the Las Vegas Plan. Folks who adhere to the Vegas Plan believe that life happens to them...and that they have no real control over their lives. Those who live by the Perspiration Plan believe that what happens depends a great deal on how hard they work...and how carefully they think. When unhappy things happen to unhappy people, they entertain a variety of thoughts that actually mire them in the muck:

- This should have never happened!
- It's not fair! I did nothing to deserve this!
- This is the end of the world.
- I never catch a break.
- Nothing I do works out!
- The only thing that helps is for everyone to know how miserable I am.

In contrast, when unhappy things happen to happy people, they allow themselves to experience sadness, grief, anger, or anxiety...but quickly begin to entertain thoughts that help them move on:

- This stinks, but I can handle it.
- Sometimes bad things happen to good people.
- Life is like a roller coaster. It won't be long before mine starts heading up!
- Even though I want to feel sorry for myself, I can't afford to.

- The best way to start feeling less negative is to start acting more positive.

While it's far easier to stay upbeat when life's serving roses rather than rotten eggs, the most dazzling difference between positive and negative people has more to do with their thinking than how much life is stinking.

Summed up, optimistic individuals understand that happiness is a choice. Therefore, they're able to weather life's inevitable storms without losing spirit. Ironically, this positive perspective leads to a self-fulfilling prophecy: People act more positively toward them! More often than not, things just seem to go their way. Will your kids have this advantage as they mature? Will they bring the best out of their coworkers and bosses? Will they be the sorts of wives, husbands, mothers, or fathers who inspire their families through love and eternal hope? This dream can come true with a little help from the Five E's of Love and Logic!

The First "E" of Love and Logic: Example

"I'm sick and tired of Tim harping on this negativity issue," Ruby ranted. "I mean, it's not like I'm that way all of the time. It's just that everything's been such a mess lately. Nothing's been going right. You should see the report cards Rachel and Ricky brought home the other day. And the neighbor parked this rusty old heap in the driveway so that we have to look at it every time we walk out the front door."

"So, Ruby," reflected her therapist, Dr. Beard, "you feel like you aren't as negative as your husband thinks you are."

"Well," she huffed, "I don't know. It just seems like I can't do anything right. Maybe I am, but he just doesn't understand how everything's been going...I don't know."

With a contemplative scratch of his goatee, Dr. Beard queried, "Would you like to know?"

"I guess," she answered. "But how?"

"Those of us who are lucky enough to have children," answered the good doctor, "have a wonderful window through which to view ourselves. Since they so closely copy our behavior and our attitudes, we can catch a glimpse of our true selves by watching them closely."

"So...if my kids act really negative, you're saying that it might mean that I'm acting really negative?"

Glancing at his watch, Dr. B empathized, "Oh goodness.... Ruby....it looks like our time is up. We'll talk about that next week. Have a good one."

"That was a dirty trick!" Ruby ruminated as she drove home from the session. "Why did he have to bring that up at the last moment?"

Like an annoying advertising jingle, it wouldn't leave her head. "Our kids copy our behavior....they're a window into ourselves...we can catch a glimpse of our true selves by watching them."

The first "E" of Love and Logic stands for Example. Parents who provide an optimistic example are far more likely to see this optimism mirrored in their children's attitudes and behavior. What do your kids hear and see you doing? Are they witnessing you complaining about clouds...or finding their silver linings? Do they observe you dwelling on others' weaknesses...or focusing on their strengths? Do they see you moping around... or making the best out of every day? Is your glass always half empty...or is it typically half full?

**Parents who provide an optimistic example
are far more likely to see this optimism mirrored in
their children's attitudes and behavior.**

Ruby wasn't pleased with what she was seeing in the mirror. "The field trip was so boring," complained Rachel, "It was totally hot on the bus, and then all we did was walk around the museum and look at old stuff."

Ricky chimed in, "At least you get to go on field trips. We never do anything fun at school."

During dinner, her reflection didn't get much brighter. "Living around here is so lame," lamented Rachel. "There's like nothing to do."

Ricky agreed, "Yeah, and all the kids around here are like big dorks."

She'd heard enough! The painful truth had begun to sink in. A sickening heaviness settled into her heart as she considered the gravity of the situation, "Maybe Tim's right. Maybe I am negative. I never do anything right."

That week was the longest of Ruby's life. As she sat in Dr. Beard's office, she couldn't help but weep, "I've ruined my kids. It's all my fault."

"What's all your fault?" Dr. B. questioned.

"Tim's right! I've been horribly negative…now my kids are even negative. I've just screwed it all up."

With a compassionate smile, he inquired, "Would you be interested in experimenting with something that might make things better?"

"What?"

Dr. B continued, "Ruby, you're not alone, and it's not all your fault. Lots of people struggle with this. Sometimes I struggle with this. From what you've told me about your parents, it's clear that you learned a great deal of positive things from them.

You also learned some negative things…like the habit of focusing on the negative."

"So…what am I supposed to do?" Ruby asked.

"Now you have a choice," he answered. "You can either choose to be a positive person or a negative one."

"Positive!" she proclaimed.

"Good!" he smiled. "Then I'd like you to imagine the most positive person you know. What does their smile look like? Do they walk with a spring in their step, or do they just drag along? What sorts of things do they typically say? How do they react when things go wrong?"

Dr. Beard knows that it's impossible to become something you can't visualize and describe. In other words, you need to see it to be it. He's also learned that the easiest way for most people to do this is to imagine someone who exemplifies the qualities they wish to acquire.

It's impossible to become something you can't visualize and describe. In other words, you need to see it to be it.

"Oh that's nauseating!" Ruby smiled, "That's Tim. He's always so upbeat that it just about makes you want to throw up. And my friend Jill is like that, too."

"Well, there you go!" Dr. B. Beamed, "You've got two examples! The second step is to spend this next week pretending to be that type of person."

"Huh?"

"Yes!" he nodded. "During this next week I want you to pretend that you're an incredibly positive person."

"Like fake it?"

"Right again!" he chuckled. "I'm asking you to fake it until you make it. People who start acting differently often start thinking and feeling differently."

Sick and tired of being sick and tired, Ruby decided to give the doctor's strange suggestion a spin. "What can I lose?" she pondered. "At least it'll get Tim off of my case."

That very afternoon, she caught herself halfway into complaining about the neighbors, "What kind of people leave a rusty old—"

Grabbing a hold of herself, she stopped in mid-sentence. Imagining what her perpetually perky husband would say, she took a u-turn and blurted, "Old cars like that really add rustic charm to the neighborhood."

Ruby couldn't believe what came out of her mouth!

Two hours later, Ricky was sitting at the table, taking a mental fiesta instead of finishing his fractions. In the past, she'd fallen into the habit of giving him the evil eye, towering over him, and ranting, "If you don't get to work, you're never going to get that done. Why don't you ever pay attention? Do you want another report card like the last one? If you keep..."

This day was different! Imagining what joyful Jill would say to her kids, she patted him on the back, smiled, and said, "Wow, Ricky! It looks like you've got your name on your paper and you've finished the first problem."

A bewildered Ricky replied, "Um...yeah?"

"There you go!" she continued with a smile. "You only have nineteen left!"

Although Ricky wasn't jumping for joy, his mother was. "It's strange," she chuckled to herself. "When I'm perky, he's too confused to argue."

The next morning was the true test of Ruby's resolve. Shaving cream smeared all over his face, Tim stood in front of the mirror whistling a sweet morning tune. "How can anybody be that happy at six in the morning?" she wondered. Although it took every bit of wherewithal she had, she plastered a smile on her face and said, "Good morning!"

Now, her husband was just as confused as her son.

As the week went by, Ruby rode a roller coaster. Sometimes she remembered to act positive. Plenty of times she didn't. Sometimes she found the strength to smile. Other times she decided that frowning was more fulfilling. Through the ups and downs, she realized what the vast majority of people do... the more positive she acted, the more positive she felt. Ruby discovered something else. When she remembered to parent in an upbeat way, her kids were far less likely to suck her into un-winnable power-struggles and arguments. Every day that went by without one of those, was a day to celebrate!

The Second "E" of Love and Logic: Expectation

"Ruby, why do you always leave such a mess? How many times do I have to tell you to clean up after yourself! Why can't you do anything right? Go to your room!"

Six-year-old Ruby sat on the rug ruminating about what just happened. As she did, she made a decision that would clang around in her head for years, "When I grow up and have my own kids, I'm going to be a nice mommy...not a mean one!"

Fifteen years later, Ruby sat on the rug playing with Rachel, her beautiful new baby. She remembered her promise, "When I'm a mommy, I'm going to be nice." And nice she was! As her bundle of joy grew and grew, Ruby spent more and more time making sure that nothing interfered with her sweet child's happiness. When two-year-old Rachel wanted to run like a banshee through the house, Ruby resisted the urge to say, "No." When Rachel jumped on the couch with her muddy little shoes, Ruby cringed, yet once again stuffed back the "No!" After all, if she was going to be a nice mommy like she promised herself, she couldn't do anything that might make her sweet Rachel upset.

Ricky hit the scene like a terrier puppy on pep pills! Now she had two tornadoes roaring though the house. Still, she had to keep her promise. "Don't be a mean mommy," she reminded herself as she watched little Ricky pour his juice down the heat register. She kept her mouth shut. "Don't be a mean mommy," she pleaded with herself as she observed Rachel go off to the first day of seventh grade in a halter top and shorts made of 100% nothing. Again, she bit her tongue. Then she watched as the two of them tussled, argued, and broke her favorite lamp. She tried to remind herself, but only half of it came out, "Don't be a..." then she blew:

For crying out loud, what's wrong with the two of you? You're driving me nuts! Why can't you just behave? Go to your rooms!

Expectation is the second "E" of Love and Logic. In her well-intentioned attempts to be the nicest mommy on the block, Ruby deprived herself and her kids of a home filled with healthy expectations. By setting no limits and giving them everything they wanted, she communicated the following:

- *The two of you aren't capable of behaving responsibly.*
- *You are the center of the world and should never have to wait for anything, work for anything, or abide by any standards.*
- *There's really no need for you to treat me...or anyone else... with respect.*

Few bosses stay up nights trying to figure out how to keep employees who believe in the "Me-Centric" theory of the universe. Most spend endless nights trying to figure out how to spot such folks during the interview process and make sure that they're never hired. An ironically sad result of keeping kids happy all of the time is that we set them up for chronic unhappiness as adults.

Life presents its fair share of inconvenience, tedium, struggle, and disappointment. Those sheltered from this as children spend their adult lives feeling disgruntled and victimized. They become the sorts of employees who wilt fresh flowers as they walk by.

Few bosses stay up nights trying to figure out how to keep employees who believe in the "Me-Centric" theory of the universe.

Those who've learned healthy ways of coping with life's trials as tots typically spend most of their lives feeling thankful for the blessings they've been given. Because they learned as kids that things don't always go their way, they aren't as bent out of shape when it happens to them as adults. The goal of every true Love and Logic parent is to make their home operate so much like the real world that their kids experience an almost seamless transition when they walk out the front door. Kids who are accustomed to limits at home become adults who are far more successful with the limits imposed by their bosses.

There's yet another sad result of providing a limit-free home: It doesn't take long before our patience wears thin. Because Ruby spent so much time trying not to be "mean" like her own mommy, she ended up parenting exactly like her mommy! Every time she allowed her kids to walk all over her, a bit more pressure built inside. Each time she kept her mouth shut...trying to be a "nice mommy"...her temperature rose. As she reached her boiling point, there weren't enough good intentions in the world to keep that lava from spewing forth. In all of her attempts to provide a perpetually calm and giving example, she ended up modeling passivity, frustration, and negativity.

Kids who are accustomed to limits at home become adults who are far more successful with the limits imposed by their bosses.

Love and Logic is a philosophy of hope and forgiveness! Is there hope for Ruby and her family? You bet! That is, only if she's willing to forgive herself and to learn some simple skills for setting and enforcing limits.

"So you're tired of being treated like a doormat by your kids," Dr. Beard replied, "but you're not sure how to turn things around."

"Yeah," Ruby replied, "I just wonder if it's too late."

"It's never too late," he smiled as he handed her a worn-out CD case. "Listen to this once a day for a week. It'll give you a few ideas...but don't try any of them until you've listened for at least a week."

As she drove home, she listened to the CD. The name of it was, "Oh, great! What do I do now?" and it talked about something called Love and Logic parenting...and what to do when your kids are on your final nerve. She giggled, laughed, and began to learn some powerful techniques for turning the tides. Sitting in her driveway with the car still running, she continued to listen. Excitement welled up inside of her, "This is crazy enough to work!"

The next morning, she remembered Dr. B.'s suggestion, "Listen to this once a day for a week." Following his advice, she listened to that same old CD six more times. Each time, she learned just a bit more. With every repetition, she also imagined in greater detail how she'd apply it with Rachel and Ricky...and how surprised they were going to be!

Saturday afternoon, Rachel raged, "Mom! Why haven't you done the wash? It's like I have nothing to wear!"

Ruby was ready to try her new skills! With calm sadness in her voice, she answered with a wonderful enforceable statement, "Oh... sweetheart...this is so sad. I'll be happy to do the extra things I do for you when I feel respected and your chores are done."

Rolling her eyes, Rachel roared, "This is so lame! My friends don't have parents that make slaves out of them."

Ruby remembered the CD and calmly replied, "I love you too much to argue about this."

"Well, it's not fair!"

Ruby stuck to her guns, "I love you too much to argue."

The next morning, Ricky yelled, "Mom! When are you going to buy something to eat around here? Where's my Carbo-Coated Sugar Pops? There's only oatmeal. I hate oatmeal! You know that I hate oatmeal!"

With practiced calmness, Mom informed him of her new work policy, "Oh...honey...I'll be happy to do the extra things I do for you when I feel respected and your chores are done."

"But I'm starving to death!" Ricky begged, "and you know that I hate oatmeal."

Remembering the voice on the CD, Ruby calmly answered, "Ricky...I love you too much to argue about this."

Horrified, he harped, "But...but...I hate oatmeal...but I'm starving..."

Walking out of the room, she softly continued, "Oh... Ricky...I love you too much to argue."

As the days passed, Ruby discovered something amazing. Her kids were happier, and so was she! "It's strange," she mused, "Kids really are happier when they have firm limits. It just takes 'em a while to get over the initial shock."

Ruby also realized that there are times when parents need to go on strike and negotiate for better working conditions. By learning just two simple statements, she transformed herself from a doormat into a powerfully positive role model:

- *I'll be happy to do the things I do for you when I feel respected and your chores are done.*
- *I love you too much to argue.*

Are you giving your kids the gift of high expectations?

The Third "E" of Love and Logic: Education

"This is the most boring, bogus neighborhood in the world," Ricky informed his mother. "There's never anything to do."

His old mother...Ruby pre-Love and Logic...would have taken the bull by the horns and launched into a never ending list of exciting endeavors: "Well, Ricky, you could go over to Evan's house and ride bikes. Then there's the pool. You could ask your sister if she wants to go. Do you have any books you like? You could read. Maybe there's something out in the garage you could work on..."

Predictable as night and day, Ricky would react, "Awe, mom. None of that stuff is fun. It's all boring."

Like a moth drawn to the flame, his old mother couldn't resist jumping head long into a debate: "Well, Ricky, you can't tell me that things are so bad here. Your father and I moved here so that you and your sister would have plenty of..."

Those were the not-so-good old days. Now Ruby was primed and ready for a far more productive approach. After studying Love and Logic, she realized that Ricky's real problem wasn't the neighborhood...but the sorts of mental habits he'd fallen into. Like a road map to unhappiness, his thinking turned everything into a downer. That's why school was stinky, his teachers were terrible, all of his friends were awful, and his life was lame.

Through her own personal journey, Ruby learned how her own negative thinking affected her life. She also learned that she had a choice about the sorts of stuff she let dance around in her head. When she allowed negative thoughts to do the tango, the world always seemed sour. When she threw them off the floor in favor of more positive ones, the sky always seemed bluer.

The Third "E" of Love and Logic stands for Education. Like any other life skill, most of how we think...and think about... is learned. Much of this education happens early in life as we closely observe our parents. If we overhear them talking positively about life, we're far more likely to develop positive thoughts and belief systems. If we see them staying upbeat in the face of adversity, we're likely to learn attitudes that allow us to do the same.

Much of this education also comes from sources outside of the home. Needless to say, our peers, teachers, and other influential people strongly influence our thinking habits. Sadly, television also appears to be the main shaping influence in the mental lives of far too many youngsters.

Ricky's new mother, Ruby post-Love and Logic, understood that he desperately needed a bit of education about the sorts of mental choices he was making. In the previous chapter, we learned five steps for guiding children to own and solve their problems. Ruby discovered that she could use these steps to help Ricky learn to solve his negativity problem. Before seeing how she does, let's review:

Step one: Provide a strong and sincere dose of empathy.
Remember that nobody cares how much you know until you show how much you care. Instead of launching into lectures, wise parents say something like, "This is so sad." Then they open their ears and listen.

Step two: Ask, "What do you think you are going to do?"
Sometimes we call this the "power message" because it communicates our belief that our kids have the strength to own and solve their problems.

Step three: When the child says, "I don't know," ask, "Would you like to hear some ideas?"
When we share control by first asking permission to provide our thoughts, our kids are far less likely to hoard control by closing their ears and minds. If your child says, "No" sidestep the power-

struggle by saying, "Thanks for being honest with me. If you change your mind, I'll be happy to share my ideas."

Step four: Give just two or three options and ask, "How will that work for you?" after each.
Remember that saying, "Some kids decide to…" is far more effective than saying, "You should…" If you suddenly find yourself stumped for ideas, just say, "I just realized that I don't have any good ideas right now. Let's talk about this later…after I've had a chance to think a bit more. Maybe you'll have some good ideas by then, too."

Also remember to help your child evaluate the possible consequences of each option by asking him, "How will that work for you?" after each.

Step five: Resist the urge to tell your child which solution to use.
Instead of telling your child which solution to use, simply say, "I know you will make a good decision on this. Good luck. Let me know how it works out."

"I don't want to go to school," Ricky complained over his breakfast. "It's like a communist dictatorship around there."

Ruby decided that there was no time like the present to go for step number one! "Wow, this is so sad," she empathized. "It must be really hard going through life thinking about how bad things are."

"What are you talking about?" Ricky pouted. "This school stinks!"

Mom continued with the empathy. "I used to dwell on how bad things are, too. I know how sad that can be. I sure hope that you can get over that habit."

"You're crazy, Mom! That's just that weird psychologist stuff."

Taking a page from Dr. Beard's training manual, she cut the session short, "Oh…look at the time…we'll talk about this tonight. Don't worry about it right now. See you after school. I love you."

Like many smart parents, Ruby realized that she didn't have to go through all five steps in one sitting. Oftentimes it's far wiser...and more practical...to spread them out a bit.

As the bus bumped along, the words Ricky's mother spoke also bumped around in his head. "What did she mean by, 'Don't worry about it right now...I hope you can get over that habit' Huh?"

Right after dinner, Ruby was ready for step two. "Ricky," she asked, "how was school?"

One word was all he could grunt, "Boring."

With a loving pat on the back, Mom replied, "Oh, there's that pesky habit again. What do you think you can do about that?"

"Mom, what are you talking about?" he groaned.

Moving on to step three, she asked, "Would you like to hear some ideas?"

"Uh...what?"

Now it was time for step four. "Well, some people decide that they kind of like feeling down all of the time. That's why they decide to just spend all of their time thinking about how bad everything is. How will that work for you?"

"Don't know," he mumbled.

"Other people realize they can make their lives happier by working really hard to find some positive things to think and say instead. How will that work?"

"That's weird, Mom."

"I only have one other idea. Some people decide that they're going to think about someone they know who is really happy. Then they just pretend to be that person for a while. They talk like they are happy, walk like they are happy, etc. These people often find out that they feel happier when they act happier. How will that work for you?"

Completely repulsed, Ricky replied, "Gall, Mom. You're freaking me out."

Rallying every erg of her self-control, Ruby rolled on to step five. With great sincerity in her voice, she replied, "Well, Ricky, I bet this does freak you out. The good thing is that you have a choice. We're going to love you the same regardless of whether you choose to be happy or choose to be sad. Good luck."

The very next day, a defeated Ruby sat in Dr. B.'s office. "How did your little problem-solving session go with Ricky?" he asked.

"Not well," she lamented. "He looked at me the whole time like I had lobsters crawling out of my ears."

"So he thought you were from another planet?" he chuckled.

"Yep, and I don't think it helped a bit," she continued.

"That's because you're just planting seeds," Dr. B. replied. "Now a little seed has been planted in Ricky's mind. If you keep setting a good example and providing high expectations, this seed will grow. Just keep watering it from time to time by reminding him that he has a choice about how he thinks and feels."

"So...you're saying that it still might work?" Ruby asked.

"You bet!" He smiled, "Many of the things we do as parents don't sprout in our children's minds until they mature a bit and have some experience with life."

"So...what do I do when I see him being negative?" Ruby asked. "Do I just keep saying these sorts of things?"

"Yes," he answered, "just keep letting him know how sad you are for him and how much you hope he will get over the habit of focusing on the negative. The main thing is that he understands that happiness is a personal choice and a personal responsibility. The vast majority of kids who understand this choose happiness in the long run."

Happiness is a personal choice and a personal responsibility. The vast majority of kids who understand this choose happiness in the long run.

The Fourth "E" of Love and Logic: Experience

Elmer and Festus are two little tykes living in the very same town on the very same street. Both have parents who adore them, and both have parents who want them to be happy. Like most tiny tykes they're happy most of the time and upset some of the time. When Elmer is happy he doesn't get much attention. When he's upset, his parents go into high gear. They're there in a flash, wiping his tears, asking him what went wrong, telling him that things will get better, feeding him ice cream, and providing parental psychotherapy. Festus's parents are quite different. When he's happy, they spend a lot of time with him talking and having fun. When he's upset, they make sure he's ok, provide a little dose of empathy, give him a quick pat on the back, and move on with what they were doing.

Which child is going to be the happiest in the long run?

There's a basic rule in psychology that goes something like the following: If we want any behavior to increase in frequency and intensity, give it plenty of attention. This attention can come in two forms...positive or negative. Ironically, the effect of each is more or less the same. Parents who provide excessive amounts of either positive or negative attention when their children are unhappy...yet give them little or no attention when they are content...run the risk of raising perpetually perturbed youngsters.

Elmer's experience is telling him that the best way to get his needs met is to be upset...and to make sure that everyone knows about it! Festus has learned just the opposite. Through experience he's learned that being unhappy just doesn't pay off.

Parents who provide excessive amounts of either positive or negative attention when their children are unhappy run the risk of raising perpetually perturbed youngsters.

The Fourth "E" of Love and Logic stands for Experience. As she drifted off to sleep that night, Ruby thought about Ricky, Rachel, and how both of them had developed the habit of spending too much time being unhappy. As she dreamed, she saw herself hovering over both of them every time they were unhappy. In her dream, they were always upset, and she was always trying to say or do something to help. Like sand running through her fingers, their happiness was ever elusive.

Ruby's dream wasn't far from the reality that used to take place in her home. As young parents with two young children, she and her husband quickly reached the limits of their endurance. Creating a utopia for their tots was a daunting duty. There just wasn't enough gas in their tanks! Doing their best to cope, each went into energy conservation mode during those brief milliseconds during which tranquility prevailed. When their kids were happy, they flopped on the couch, closed their eyes, and caught their breath. When any drama unfolded, they were quick to jump to their feet and give it their undivided attention.

Is there any hope for parents who've fallen into this unhealthy habit with their kids? Definitely! It just takes two simple steps to turn things around:

- When your kids are content, describe what you see them doing and provide plenty of eye contact, smiles, and touch.
- When your kids are unhappy, provide a quick dose of empathy and hand the problem back.

Ruby and her husband Tim understood that they needed to apply this first step far more frequently. Getting out of the habit of ignoring happiness and hovering over unhappiness wasn't going to be easy. That's why they needed some sort of systematic way of reminding themselves to focus more on the positive. As a starting goal, each agreed that they would intentionally attend to at least three instances of joy during the first week. Taking it a step farther, Ruby wrote her name right next to Tim's on a small slip of paper. "Every time I pay attention to them when they're happy," she said to her husband, "I'll put a check under my name. Will you do the same?"

Tim, being naturally perky from birth, chimed, "Sure, honey. Then we can tape that up on our mirror to remind us...and whoever gets the most checks wins!"

"Honey, I'm really trying to be more positive these days," she moaned, "but your thing about who gets the most checks wins is...well...annoying."

"Well, okay," he giggled, "we can just tape it on the mirror to remind us."

"Fine," Ruby replied.

Unable to contain the child within, Tim continued, "But if I get the most you get to take me out to dinner."

"This is going to be a long week," Ruby replied.

Monday morning, Ruby saw that little slip of paper and remembered her goal. That evening, she saw Rachel giggling with a friend on the phone. "This is the perfect time!" Ruby thought. "When she gets off the phone, I'll go for it."

Approaching her adolescent daughter, she smiled, looked her in the eye, patted her on the back, and said, "You really like talking to your friends on the phone."

Rachel's confused response was less than enthusiastic, "Mom, you are like so weird. Like what?"

Ruby just smiled, "Oh honey. I was worried that I might be weird."

Rachel countered, "Well...like...you are."

With another smile and pat on the back, Ruby teased, "And the very sad thing for you...sweetie...is that weirdness is genetic. It's passed down from mothers to daughters."

Tuesday morning, that slip of paper once again spoke to Ruby. "Remember me? Don't forget to notice some happiness today!"

Looking out the window, she saw Ricky doing skateboard tricks in the driveway. Storming out the front door, she thought, "This is great!"

Looking into his eyes, smiling, and going for a high five, Ruby said, "It looks like you've been working on some new tricks!"

Too surprised to be snippy, Ricky replied, "Uh yeah. Wanna see the one I just figured out?"

Thinking how much better this felt than spending all of her time trying to mop up distress, she answered, "You bet!"

By the end of the week, it wasn't clear whether Ruby or Tim had the most check marks. What was clear to both of them was that everybody was a winner. Ruby had more energy, Tim had a happier wife, and the kids were beginning to learn from experience that they don't need to have a crisis to get the attention they crave.

The Fifth "E" of Love and Logic: Empathy

Let's review. In the previous section, Ruby learned that one way of teaching our kids that being happy is more productive than being upset is to avoid giving the lion's share of attention to soap opera-like behavior. She also learned two practical skills for doing this:

- When your kids are content, describe what you see them doing and provide plenty of eye contact, smiles, and touch.
- When your kids are unhappy, provide a quick dose of empathy and hand the problem back.

She tackled this first skill with relative ease. All it took were some attainable goals and a little slip of paper to remind her of these goals. The second skill was proving a bit more difficult. Like most parents, her heart truly ached when her children were upset. Because of this, she found herself owning all of their problems. In fact, things often became so twisted around that she found herself being more upset and worried about their problems than they were! As she came to understand Love and Logic, she learned that this wasn't doing her kids any favors. Instead, it was sending the message that they weren't capable of coping with life's challenges.

Many youngsters suffer from the "no sense in all of us worrying about it" syndrome. This horribly debilitating condition occurs when their parents expend more energy working and worrying about their problems than they do. Looking around, they reason, "My parents are really, really worried about my life. They're working their tails off solving my problems. No sense in all of us worrying about this, it looks like they've got it handled!"

Many youngsters suffer from the "no sense in all of us worrying about it" syndrome. This horribly debilitating condition occurs when their parents expend more energy working and worrying about their problems than they do.

It's at this precise point in time that their mental gears come to a grinding halt. Early in their lives, Ricky and Rachel learned that their mother would do all their worrying and work for them. As a result, they weren't exceptionally enthusiastic when she started making some healthy changes. They grew particularly perturbed when she really began to understand the difference between empathy and sympathy.

In the past, Ruby reacted to their problems in the following way: "Mom," Ricky would scream, "somebody stole my bike."

With horror painted all over her face, she'd respond, "This is horrible. How did it happen? Did you lock it up?"

With tears welling in his eyes, Ricky would whine, "I forgot… and I thought it was ok…and I was in a hurry to get to class… and the combination is so hard to remember…and…and…my teacher gets so mad when I'm late."

"This is terrible." she'd continue, "Your school really needs to have a more secure place for kids to keep their bikes."

Sniffling, Ricky would agree, "Yeah. Nobody even watches them for you. They don't even care."

Roaring into full rescue mode, she'd rant, "Well. I'm not very happy about having to buy you another one, but let's go. The sporting goods store is open until nine."

Was Mom's old approach empathetic or sympathetic? What's the difference? Years ago, when I was trudging through my training as a psychologist, one of my wisest professors told us a little story. In this story, a man was hiking up a narrow mountain trail. As he reached the top, he lost his footing and began to slide off of a sheer cliff. Desperately grasping for a lifeline, he managed to grab a tree root protruding from the cliff. A roaring river raged five hundred feet below his feet. There he hung, screaming for his life.

Another hiker heard his cries for help. Racing up the trail, he located the desperate man and shouted, "Hold on. I'll be right there!" Sliding down the cliff, he grabbed a hold of the tree root and hung right next to the bewildered and dismayed gentleman. Now both of them were in the same fix!

Hearing their cries for help, a third hiker arrived on the scene. Being quite wiser than the first "rescuer," he shouted, "Hold on. I'll tie this rope to a strong tree and lower the other end down to you." As he did, the two men pulled themselves to safety.

So…what's the moral to this story? In the past, Ruby had been like the first hiker to the "rescue." Instead of helping her children pull themselves out of their problems, she'd leap over the cliff and make their problems hers. This behavior, my wise professor taught, is the epitome of sympathy: Becoming so involved in others' problems that they become yours...and everybody ends up suffering.

Now that she was learning to replace crippling sympathy with empowering empathy, Ruby began to personify the second rescuer on the scene. Instead of jumping over the cliff each time her children had a problem, she was learning to show concern while giving them the tools for life-long success. And it wasn't long before she had plenty of opportunities to apply her new skills.

> **Instead of jumping over the cliff each time her children had a problem, she was learning to show concern while giving them the tools for life-long success.**

Believe it or not, Ricky's second bike also ended up missing! This time Ruby was ready to throw him a rope instead of a shiny new mountain bike.

"Mom!" Ricky screamed into the phone, "you need to come and get me! Somebody stole my bike!"

Resisting the urge to rant, rave, and rescue, Ruby answered, "Oh, this is so sad. What are you going to do?"

"Mom!" Ricky continued, "somebody stole my bike! It wasn't my fault. I was in a hurry."

"Oh, this is so sad," repeated Ruby. "It's going to take me a while to get over there. This will give you plenty of time to figure out how you are going to afford another. Try not to worry about it too much right now. I love you."

As his mother was driving him home from the school, Ricky complained, "It wasn't my fault. Don't you know that this is a high crime area? When are we going to get another one? I need something to ride to school."

Ruby was ready, "Oh, this is so sad. You may have another as soon as you can afford one."

Ricky was shocked, "But...but...but..."

Mom continued, "Would you like to hear what some kids do when this happens?"

"What?" Ricky asked with disgust.

His mother was actually having fun. "Some kids decide to just ride the bus. How would that work for you?"

Ricky was double disgusted, "Awe, mom! It takes forever to get home and all of the kids are such dorks."

"Other kids," she continued, "decide go to the thrift store and see if there are any used ones down there. How would that work?"

Triple disgusted, Ricky moaned, "All of those are old and the gears don't work."

Sharing just one more idea, Ruby suggested, "Some kids decide to do a bunch of extra jobs around home and the neighborhood so that they can save up enough money to buy the kind of bike they really want. How would that work?"

Quadruple disgusted, Ricky grunted, "Gall! Nobody cares. I thought you loved me."

Sealing the deal, Ruby patted him on the back and said, "I really hope this works out for you. Good luck."

As Ricky and Rachel grew, Ruby noticed something exciting. The more problems they solved, they more positive about life they became. The first time this hit her over the head was the day that Ricky rolled up the sidewalk on the brand new bike he'd earned through his own sweat and tears. The smile on his face was wider than the Mississippi River, and the twinkle in his eyes sparkled brighter than fine diamonds. There he sat...the personification of happiness. Never before was it clearer to Ruby that true happiness comes from doing great things...rather than being given them.

**True happiness comes from doing great things…
rather than being given them.**

CHAPTER FOUR

Great Mistakes!

Show your kids how to learn from their mistakes rather than repeat them.

Mr. Romano and his wife are ready for a well-earned vacation from their hardware store business. It's about time they took a little break! Ten years ago, they started the store with a pocket full of cash, a small business loan, and lots of sweat and tears. Now it's thriving, and they've got an extremely conscientious young man at the management helm. While George has never run the store in their absence, he's been on board for two years and has learned quickly. Mr. Romano believes that he's ready to take charge while they spend a couple of weeks soaking up the sun and fun in Acapulco.

At Romano's Hardware Haven, the phone is already ringing off of the hook by seven Monday morning. It's Mr. Copper, their plumbing supplier. "We've got a truck load of pipe, six cases of three-quarter elbows, a dozen traps, and ten of them fancy bathroom faucets. Do you want the gold finish on all of them faucets or just half? And Romano said he wanted some of the water-saver heads. How many should I pack? I can't get the price I originally quoted on those, but I can still do retail minus thirty percent. Will that work?"

George is a careful, conscientious young man, and the last thing he wants to do is make a mistake. "Uh, Mr. Romano won't be back until the thirtieth. Umm…he didn't say anything about this. I'm not sure what he wanted. Can you wait until he gets back?"

Just a few minutes later, a customer walks in carrying a voltage tester. "This darn thing doesn't work. It reads six volts even when it isn't even plugged in. Here's my receipt."

George is a careful guy. The last thing he wants to do is make a mistake. "Uh, we aren't supposed to accept returns on electrical items."

"You got to be kidding! I spend money here every day, and you won't take back a lousy ten dollar tester?"

George wants to help, but he doesn't want to blow it. "I'm really sorry, but Mr. Romano is out until the thirtieth, we aren't supposed to accept returns of electrical items. Maybe you can talk to him when he gets back."

At one-o-clock, Ms. Addison of the Daily Times is on line two. "I have a question on this ad you wanted to place for your spring sale. Do you want that headline font in bold or all caps? I faxed over a couple samples, and I need to get your thoughts so that this can go out on the seventeenth."

As you know, George is a careful conscientious young man. By now, you also know that he'd rather lose an arm than make a mistake. "Yeah, I received those samples. I'm not sure which would be best. Mr. Romano won't be back until the thirtieth, and he didn't say which he wanted. Uh, what's the deadline on that? I can see if I can get a hold of him and get back to you."

A note is slipped on George's desk near the end of the day, "We're out of ten penny nails!"

George wonders, "I know that I could order some through Steele Brothers…but there's J and J Wholesalers…"

You already know what George fears the most. Instead of getting hammered forward, the nail order gets tacked on the back burner... just like everything else over the next thirteen business days.

Mr. Romano and his wife are tan and happy. That is, until they find out that George hasn't made a single decision over the past two weeks. At Hardware Haven, things are gummed up worse than the bottom of an old movie theatre seat. What a mess! The careful young man they'd hired with such great expectations taught them some very costly lessons. "Isn't it strange?" They thought. "The thing that seemed to be George's greatest strength turned into his greatest weakness. And it's ironic. In all his efforts to avoid making mistakes, he made the greatest of them all...not making any."

Our great nation was founded by folks who were risk takers. They weren't afraid of making some mistakes. The future of America depends on us raising young people who possess this same spirit.

Our great nation was founded by folks who were risk takers. They weren't afraid of making some mistakes. The future of America depends on us raising young people who possess this same spirit.

My heart aches for all of the Georges in the world, who're so afraid of goofing that they never learn or achieve a thing. We all know that the road to wisdom is paved with mistakes. One of the most profound differences between those who've become highly successful and those who haven't is the quantity of mistakes made by each. Successful folks make far more blunders than their less successful peers. That's right! Those who achieve greatness are those who aren't afraid to take calculated risks, make manageable mistakes, and learn from them. They see life as a scientific laboratory, full of exciting experiments. Each decision made is simply a hypothesis to be tested. All bear the fruit of wisdom.

Would the world have ended if George ordered the wrong faucets? Or would he have learned a great deal? Would the sky have fallen if he'd allowed a return on an item that he shouldn't have? Nope! Would Mr. Romano have fired him if he'd chosen bold font instead of all caps for their ad headline? It's not likely! There's great truth in the old cliché, "Nothing risked, nothing gained." Those who grow up believing that mistakes are horrible suffer major disadvantages in the work world:

- Because they fear failure so much, they never try anything that they might not be able to do perfectly.
- When things go wrong, they quickly become discouraged and give up.
- Instead of experimenting with fresh solutions to problems, they cling to their security blanket of stale strategies.
- Whenever their work environment or responsibilities change in any way, they become fearful and stressed.
- They watch their more adventurous coworkers pass them by for pay raises and promotions.
- As time goes by, they experience more discouragement and burnout.

Conversely, those who believe that small errors offer opportunities for great insights experience the following advantages:

- Because they understand that mistakes lead to wisdom, they aren't afraid to learn new things.
- When things go wrong, they learn from them and keep trying.
- Instead of staying mired in conceptual quick sand, they aren't afraid to think "outside of the box" and experiment with fresh solutions to problems.

- Whenever their work environment or responsibilities change in any way, they get excited and energized.
- They rise to the top of their professions.
- As time goes by, they gain more enjoyment out of work… and life.

So, what's the secret to giving our children these gifts? Again, the Five E's of Love and Logic provide a wealth of practical practices.

The First "E" of Love and Logic: Example

The Petersons were perplexed by their ten-year-old son, Peter. Wringing their hands, they wondered and worried, "Why is he such a perfectionist? He won't try a thing unless he can do it perfectly. What's going to become of our dear son Peter?"

Later that evening, Mrs. Peterson smelled pot roast burning in the oven. Dumping its smoldering remains in the sink, she pouted, "I just can't do anything right! Why didn't I set the timer? Now dinner's ruined."

A pensive Peter sat near by, soaking up the smell of their charred dinner…as well as the sight of his dear mother's despair.

The next day, Mr. Peterson raced through the house, searching for his lost car keys. "Why is it," he ranted, "that I can never find those things when I need them? I must be losing my mind! If I wasn't so stupid, I'd put them some place I could find them!"

Again, Peter sat near by, carefully listening and watching.

Mr. and Mrs. Green live next door to the Petersons. While the Petersons worry about their pensive Peter, the Greens can barely keep up with their go-getter Gary. Sitting across the table from his fifth grade teacher, they listen with pride. "Gary is one of my most enthusiastic students!" beams Ms. Bunn, "There isn't a thing he's afraid tackle. He jumps right in!"

On the way home, Gary sat smiling in the back seat. As they neared their home, the car began to spit and sputter. "What's wrong?" Mrs. Green asked as her husband carefully guided the car to a safe resting spot.

Red with embarrassment, Mr. Green mumbled, "Uh...well... I think I just learned something." Pointing at the instrument panel, he continued, "You see...this car just seems to run a whole lot better when I pay attention and make sure that the needle right there stays above the 'E'!"

In the back seat, Gary soaks up a little lesson about cars, gas gauges, and paying attention so that you have enough fuel to get where you're going. The much larger lesson he learns is that mistakes offer precious opportunities for life-long learning.

The very next day, Mrs. Green goofs. Running into the house with a huge wet spot all over her pants, she announces, "Hey, Gary! I learned something today. I learned that humans have a special protection reflex when they get scared."

"What's that?" Gary inquired.

"Well," she replied, "When you get scared, your legs automatically squeeze together."

"Huh?" Gary queried.

Mom continued, "Well, I learned that if you're sitting in your car with a big cup of soda between your legs...and somebody pulls out in front of you in another car...your legs automatically squeeze together...and the lid pops off...and all of that soda and ice goes all over you."

"That's good!" Gary giggled.

Mom continued, "I learned something else, sweetie. When it gushes all over you, it's really cold!"

As you know, the First "E" of Love and Logic stands for Example. When our youngsters witness us woefully cursing our blunders...and beating up on ourselves...they learn from example that mistakes are to be avoided like the plague. Little Peter

Peterson learned early in his life that "big people" hate making all of those horrible mistakes. Since all tots yearn to become "big" like their parents, Peter planned a safe route toward an error-free life.

Little Gary Green developed a different mindset. Watching the "big people" in his life, he learned from example that big people learn from mistakes. Unlike Peter, Gary decided early in life that he would become "big" someday by learning from his bloopers. "Someday," he'd often muse, "I'll mess up enough to be as smart as my mom and dad!"

If you've fallen into the habit of beating up on yourself or displaying dismay every time you make a mistake, it's never too late to turn things around! The Petersons listened with interest as Mrs. Lovejoy, Peter's teacher, conveyed some compassionate suggestions. "In my thirty-five years of teaching, I've met plenty of children like Peter. One of the best things about them is that they're so careful. Unfortunately, this can also be their greatest weakness. They often become too careful to try anything new or difficult. Fortunately, there is something that you can do to help."

Feeling a spark of hope, the Petersons prodded, "What is it? What can we do?"

With a warm smile that felt like a hug, Mrs. Lovejoy answered, "Make lots and lots of mistakes in front of Peter."

"So that he sees that it's ok?" asked Mr. Peterson.

"Oh yes!" Mrs. Lovejoy replied with another smile, "When you make those mistakes let him overhear you saying things like, 'I sure did learn from that!' or 'Oh, well. Everybody makes mistakes. That's how we learn.'"

"I find it pretty easy to make mistakes!" joked Mrs. Peterson.

"We all do!" Mrs. Lovejoy agreed. "The hard part is handling them in way that shows our children that it's not the end of the world when we do."

The very next day, the Petersons decided to put the plan in action. "Guess what I learned today, honey?" Mr. Peterson asked his lovely wife.

"What?" she questioned.

He answered with a grin, "I learned that blue and black look the same in the dark."

"Really?"

"Oh yes!" he announced. "When I got to work I realized that I was wearing a black shoe on one foot and a dark blue one on the other. We all got a kick out of that!"

"I bet!" she laughed.

"Yep!" he said. "I think I'm going to start paying closer attention to my feet before I leave the house!"

"That's a good idea!" Peter laughed from across the room.

Remembering their conversation with Mrs. Lovejoy, Dad smiled at Peter, patted him on the back, and proclaimed, "Yes! I guess that's the way we all learn…by making lots and lots of mistakes."

Setting a good example for our kids doesn't mean trying to be perfect. Isn't that a comforting thought! It simply means doing our best to show our kids that each goof-up is an opportunity for growth.

Setting a good example for our kids doesn't mean trying to be perfect. It simply means doing our best to show our kids that each goof-up is an opportunity for growth.

The Second "E" of Love and Logic: Expectation

Liz and her husband Lester purchased practically every parenting book published. Reading each and every page with great care, they digested theory after theory…and technique after technique. Sure, they weren't even parents yet, but they wanted to be prepared. You never know when that stork might land on your roof!

And land he did…with twins! They were overjoyed. Standing over their lovely duo, they thought, "Our children aren't going to misbehave and mess up like other people's kids. We've read all of those books! All we have to do is apply what we've learned." All was right with the world. Liz and Lester were ready for any sort of parenting perplexity.

Bernie and Bernice were the sweetest little babies in the whole world. There was just one problem. As they started to grow, they started doing naughty things. When two-year-old Bernie spit beats across the table, Liz and Lester were confused. When Bernice flushed dad's wallet down the toilet, their shock grew to epic proportions. "This can't be!" they thought. "We read all of those books and used all of those theories. Why are our kids messing up and misbehaving?"

Over the next few years, their feelings of shock and confusion turned into frustration, anger, and self-defeat. By the time Bernie and Bernice jumped on the school bus for their first day of first grade, Liz and Lester were at the end of their rope. "Why are our kids still messing up and misbehaving?" they pleaded. "We read all of those books and used all of those theories!"

The second "E" of Love and Logic stands for Expectation. In the previous chapters, we've learned the following:

- Children live up to…or down to…our expectations.
- When we believe that our kids are capable of behaving responsibly, our verbal and nonverbal behavior communicates this expectation.
- High expectations are firmly established when we set limits with Enforceable Statements.
- High expectations are also conveyed when we guide children

to own and solve their problems instead of bailing them out every time they blow it.

In this chapter, we're looking at a slightly different type of expectation...our expectation about what's going to happen when we apply effective parenting techniques. Over the past thirty years, we've noticed something about the vast majority of books and articles on parenting. While many are very good, most seem to convey the following message:

If you use these theories and techniques correctly, your kids will no longer misbehave or mess up.

When we approach parenting with this sort of expectation, we're destined for a life of frustration and disappointment. Why? Because kids will misbehave and mess up regardless of what we do. In fact, we certainly hope that they do! In every book, article, audio, and video we've produced, we've made a concerted effort to send a much different message than the books read by Liz and Lester:

If you use what we teach, your kids will continue to mess up... and that's great! With these techniques you can help them learn from their mistakes when the price tag is still small.

At the risk of annoying the daylights out of you, I'm going to say it again. Children are far better off when they are:

• allowed to make plenty of small mistakes when they are young
• held accountable for the consequences of such mistakes

This is done in a firm yet empathetic way.

Far too many parents develop the expectation that being a good parent means making sure that your kids never goof up. As a result, they rob their children of inexpensive learning experiences. They fail to realize that it's far better for their child to break a toy by playing carelessly at age three than break themselves by playing carelessly as a teen or young adult.

There's another benefit associated with praying for affordable mistakes: We aren't nearly as upset when they happen! Liz and Lester set themselves up for getting angry and frustrated by entertaining the expectation that they'd be able to parent in such a precise way that their twins would never misbehave or mess up. Strangely, this expectation actually paves the way for more mistakes and bad behavior.

Because Liz and Lester were so focused on achieving perfection with their little Bernice and Bernie, they found themselves becoming more and more upset each time they misbehaved. When children see us displaying anger and frustration over their behavior, they begin to slip into the Misbehavior Cycle:

Child Experiments With Misbehavior
I wonder what will happen if I try this?

Child Begins to Feel Hopeless	**Parent Gets Frustrated and Angry**
I'm so bad that the adults in my life can't even make me behave.	*This sort of thing really makes us mad! Why can't you just behave?*

Child Develops Disrespect for Authority Figures
If these people find it this frustrating to make me behave, they must not be very strong.

101

As you can see, each time our kids see us getting angry and frustrated, they become more and more hopeless about their ability to behave. Many also come to realize that each time they act up they gain control over their parents' emotions. It's as if they reason, "Look at me! Even though I'm just a little kid, I can change the color of my daddy's face!" There's nothing more rewarding to a strong-willed child than this feeling of excitement and control. The more frequently this cycle spins, the less respect children have for adults...and themselves.

There's another benefit associated with praying for affordable mistakes: We aren't nearly as upset when they happen!

When Liz and Lester first heard the name "Love and Logic" from the pastor of their church, they didn't buy it for a minute. "That's nuts!" Lester commented. "Love and logic? How in the world do those two things go together?"

Liz agreed, "It must be some of that hippie stuff."

Pastor Joe just laughed and replied, "Well, just do me a favor and listen to this CD called The Four Steps to Responsibility. If nothing else it'll make you laugh."

As Liz and Lester listened to the CD, they were pleasantly surprised. "This stuff actually makes sense!" uttered an astounded Lester.

Liz just put her index finger over her mouth and said, "Shhhh! I'm trying to listen."

From plenty of past experience, Lester had learned to pay attention any time he was shushed by his wife. As he listened to the CD, he realized that both of them had been beating up on themselves for having normal kids who act up. He also realized that their kids needed to play catch-up in the mistake-making department.

That night Lester stumbled sleepily into the kitchen where Liz sat at the table. "What's wrong? Why are you awake?"

"I couldn't sleep," she replied

"What are you doing?" he asked. "What are you writing at this time of the night?"

"I couldn't stop thinking about how the kids need to make more mistakes," she answered."

Rubbing the sleep from his eyes, he continued, "But what are you writing?"

"I thought it might be good to write some goals for the kids…you know…the mistakes that they need to make."

"In the middle of the night?" he asked.

"I know it's weird," she admitted, "but I couldn't stop thinking about it. I'm afraid I'll forget if I don't write something down."

Glancing at the tablet, Lester read Liz's list:

Some of the mistakes our kids need to make from time to time…

- Forget to do their chores
- Forget to bring their lunch money to school
- Waste their allowance
- Break one of their favorite toys
- Refuse to pick up their toys
- Forget to do their homework
- Do some of their homework wrong
- Get a few bad grades
- Argue, whine or talk back
- Track mud into the house
- Act up a bit at school
- Act up a bit at recess
- Act up a bit on the bus
- Decide to carry their coats on a cold day…instead of wearing them
- Lose their coats, hats, or gloves
- Do a crumby science fair project
- Act up in the store or restaurant
- Argue and tussle with each other in the back seat of the car

- Refuse to eat what I serve them
- And more…

Bernice and Bernie are very lucky kids. With all of these learning opportunities, they'll have Ph.D.s in wisdom by age eighteen! Their parents are lucky, too! Because they now understand that mistakes are more precious than gold, they won't be nearly as upset when they happen.

The Third "E" of Love and Logic: Education

The horrific look on her face signaled to me that something I just said may have touched a nerve. The other parents in the seminar seemed fairly content, but she obviously wasn't. "Dr. Fay," she questioned, "are you telling me that you'd just stand by as your kids made mistakes?"

My initial response was slightly less than brilliant, "Uh… well…um."

She continued, "It just doesn't seem right!"

"I think you're right about that!" I agreed. "It just doesn't seem natural, does it?"

"No!" she proclaimed, "How will they know to avoid making mistakes if we don't explain the consequences?"

The third "E" of Love and Logic stands for Education. Many parents…and parenting "experts"…believe that it's wise to spend copious amounts of time telling kids exactly what they should be learning from each and every experience. We disagree. While it's critical to educate our children about life and the consequences of mistakes, parents who rely on "educational lectures," demands, and threats typically end up with kids who ignore them and do unwise things behind their backs. More successful parents educate through example…and by sharing well-timed information about possible consequences.

Before I describe what I mean by sharing "well-timed information about possible consequences," let's get real. There's just no substitute for common sense! Some mistakes are simply too costly to sit back and allow our kids to make.

**When a child is in imminent danger,
forget everything you've learned in parenting books
and do whatever you can to protect her!**

If you see your child about to run in front of a speeding truck, yank them back onto the sidewalk and give them a good old-fashioned "talking-to." If you see them riding their skateboards without wearing helmets, demand their boards, and don't give them back until they agree to protect their brains. If your kid wants clothes that look like those worn by a local gang, tell them why and refuse to buy them. If you become aware that your child is using alcohol or drugs, explain your concerns, call the police and get them professional help. The list goes on and on.

Fortunately, there are plenty of missteps our kids can make without losing life or limb. These are the sorts of things our good friend Liz listed above. When these wonderful opportunities arise, Love and Logic parents follow these steps:

- Whenever your child is about to make an affordable mistake, say, "Oooo, I'm not sure I'd do that."
- Give your child a brief description of what might happen to you if you made the mistake. In other words, share some "well-timed information about possible consequences."
- Quickly shut your mouth and allow them to goof anyway.
- Allow them to learn by experiencing your empathy paired with logical consequences.
- Resist the urge to say, "I told you so!"

There they sat, making sculptures out of their mashed potatoes and green beans.

Bernie whined, "I hate mashed potatoes."

Bernice begged, "Yeah, why can't we have something else?"

Liz replied with an enforceable statement, "Dinner is served until seven thirty. Just get what you need to hold you until breakfast."

Bernie wasn't impressed, "Awe man, I'm not eating this."

Bernice agreed, "Yuck. Not me neither."

About to launch into another "There are starving kids in China" lecture, Mom grabbed herself and used a little Love and Logic, "Oooo, I don't think I'd miss dinner. I might get really hungry."

Like any other child worth keeping, Bernie shook his head and replied, "I won't be hungry."

Bernice agreed with her brother, "Not me neither."

When we describe what might happen to us...AND...we allow our kids to make the mistake anyway, we up the odds of them viewing us with renewed respect. For example, if I say to my child, "I don't think I'd buy that toy. It doesn't look well made...but, I guess you can decide since it's your money," I give him an opportunity to learn.

If he buys the toy and it breaks the very next day, he's forced to reason, "Dang, my dad knew that was going to happen! He might just know what he's talking about."

If time goes by and I say, "Gosh, I don't think I'd loan my bike to Dennis. It might get beat up," and Dennis trashes the two-wheeler, my kiddo has another opportunity to see me as being the wisest father on earth. It won't take long before he learns to listen very carefully to my "well-timed information."

The Fourth "E" of Love and Logic: Experience

Remembering that kids don't learn from the mistakes they aren't allowed to make, Liz looked at little Bernie and Bernice and replied, "Like I said, I think I'd get hungry if I missed dinner. But...since you know your tummies better than I do, I guess you're the ones who need to decide how much to put in them."

Bernie beamed, "Yeah, mommy. My tummy is ok."

Bernice agreed, "Yep, my tummy doesn't need more."

All was right with the world...until later that evening.

Kids don't learn from the mistakes they aren't allowed to make.

The fourth "E" of Love and Logic stands for Experience. When our kids blow it, it's awfully tempting to remind them how brilliant we are. Yep, it's hard to resist the urge to describe how much better things would have turned out if they'd just listened. Sadly, parents who can't resist this urge end up destroying the learning opportunity...as well as their relationships with their kids.

Great wisdom comes from experiencing the consequences of our poor decisions...not from being lectured about what we should have done instead.

Bernice and Bernie begged, "We're starving to death! We're so hungry. We need something to eat!"

In the past, Lester would've gone right through the ceiling, "Of course you are hungry! I told you this was going to happen! See...I tell you and I tell you. How many times do I have to tell you that you need to eat enough the first time? Okay...I know you're hungry... so I'll make you peanut butter and jelly sandwiches. But this is the last time!"

This time he resisted this urge, locking in the empathy instead, "Oh, no...I hate feeling that way."

Sniffling, they agreed, "Yeah, it's horrible."

Lester continued, "Well…your plates from dinner are still in the refrigerator. Help yourselves."

A bewildered Bernie replied, "But it's cold…and we hate mashed potatoes."

Bernice nodded, "Yeah. We hate them."

With a warm hug, Lester stuck to his guns, "I know it's hard. Hang in there."

"But that's mean," Bernie sobbed.

"Yeah, you're a mean daddy," Bernice concurred. "We're probably going to die."

Papa wasn't about to get sucked into that one. "Oh, guys. We talked to the doctor, and he told us that there's never been a documented case of kids dying from eating cold leftovers. I love you."

That evening, Bernice and Bernie were learning that wisdom doesn't come with candy coating. To gain enough of it to survive and enjoy success, we've got to swallow some bitter pills along the way.

The very next evening, the twins sat at the table complaining about their meat loaf and peas.

With a face twisted up tighter than a Timex, Bernie whined, "I don't like this. It's got black stuff on it."

As usual, Bernice nodded and aligned with her beloved brother. "Yeah. What's that little black stuff? It looks like bugs!"

Liz kept her cool. Instead of saying what she really wanted to say, she calmly replied, "That's ok. Maybe the two of you will like what we have for breakfast better."

The twins weren't about to give in without a fight. "Yeah, but why can't you make us something better?"

Liz, resisting the urge to bring up last night's hunger strike, stroked their little egos, "You are such good thinkers! I just know you'll be able to decide whether to eat what's served or wait until breakfast."

"You don't care if we get hungry," Bernie moaned.

Bernice nodded, "Yeah, you're a mean mommy."

Liz kept repeating, "I love you guys too much to argue."

As they stared at their rapidly cooling meals, a little voice in their heads began to pipe up, "Do you remember last night? You didn't eat your dinner. Then you got really hungry. Then your mommy and daddy didn't give in…even after you whined, begged, and had a fit. What do you think is going to happen if you make that same mistake again?"

Wisdom doesn't often come with candy coating. Instead, we've got to swallow some bitter pills along the way.

Something truly ironic happens when we resist the urge to remind kids about the consequences of their previous poor decisions. They're far more likely to remind themselves! When they don't hear our voice nagging them about what they should have learned, it's far easier for them to develop their own voice that helps them stay on the straight and narrow.

All of us have a very strong need to feel competent…to believe that we can learn from the consequences of our good and not-so-good choices. When we say to our children, "Do you remember what happened last time? Do you remember how sad you were? Do you want that to happen again? Have you learned your lesson?" we communicate the following expectation:

You're too slow to learn from your mistakes.

In contrast, if we can keep our mouths shut, we send a far more positive expectation about their competence:

What a brilliant young person you are!

As we already know, our children either live up to…or down to…our expectations. In just two evenings, Bernie and Bernice learned two critically important things: First, it's a really long time between dinner and breakfast when your tummy is empty. Second, meatloaf doesn't taste so bad if you drown it in ketchup and swallow little bits without chewing.

The Fifth "E" of Love and Logic: Empathy

Standing up in the middle of my presentation, she shouted, "Sure, this all makes sense when kids forget their lunch…or break some cheap toy…or act up a little bit at school, but how do you do all of this when kids make mistakes that aren't on the list?"

The entire audience looked at her. Then they looked at me. On the spot, I stumbled, "Uh…so what…so what list?"

"You know," she replied. "That list you talk about. That list of mistakes that it's good for kids to make. What do you do if they make mistakes that aren't on that list?"

"Well…" I began to answer, "if they—"

Cutting me short, she continued, "Like I have this friend who found drugs in her kid's room. How do you stay all calm and empathetic when something like that happens? Or, how does my friend do it when her kid just says, 'You can't tell me what to do!' and goes out at night without her permission?"

Over the years I've been utterly amazed by how many people have "friends" with these sorts of problems.

As you know by now, the fifth "E" of Love and Logic stands for Empathy. In previous chapters, we learned that empathy is the key to helping our kids learn from the consequences of their actions. It's the empathy that allows them to think more about their bad decisions than how bad we are. It's the empathy that leaves them thinking, "I've got a major problem!" rather than, "What's my parent's problem?"

With all of this said, how's a parent apply this powerful skill when their kids make mistakes that leave them feeling anxious, overwhelmed, or downright fit-to-be-tied? For years I tried to teach people how to apply empathy when they were upset and angry. For years I was frustrated by the fact that they weren't learning. "What's wrong with them?" I wondered. "Nothing!" was my final conclusion.

I couldn't even do it myself. That's right! Despite my valiant attempts to teach others to use empathy when they were angry, I couldn't do it. Every time I tried, it came across as sarcastic or phony. Of course, I didn't think it was sarcastic, but everybody else who heard it did. I suppose the hallmark of growing maturity is the willingness to trust others' opinions even when you know they're wrong.

Instead of trying to use empathy when I was upset or angry, I began to realize that it's far more helpful to give myself permission not to use it. Yep, at times like this, it's far more productive and practical to delay the consequence by saying…

I'm too angry to think straight! I make better decisions when I'm calm. I'm going to do something about this later.

Does this buy you time to calm down?

Does this give you a chance to get some help and support from others?

Does this give you an opportunity to think of an appropriate, logical consequence?

Does this allow you to practice your empathy so that you're sure it will come across sincere?

Is this good modeling?

Would America be a more peaceful and productive place if kids were seeing more adults taking time to think before they reacted in anger?

Anyone who's used this skill with children knows what a lifesaver it can be. Regardless of how skilled and intelligent we may be, there will always be those times when our kids leave us completely lost for words...at least the types of words we can be proud of.

Would America be a more peaceful and productive place if kids were seeing more adults taking time to think before they reacted in anger?

Anyone who's managed adults also understands the power of this skill. Countless times in my professional life with employees I've found myself in situations such as these...situations where I was tempted to rant and rave rather than keep my cool. One specific situation always comes to mind when I think about the power of delayed consequences. I always remember the employee who thought it wise to say, "This is stupid! You can't tell me what to do!" when I calmly asked her to cut down on the number of personal calls she was making during working hours.

Before I go into the details, there's a myth we need to dispel. This familiar fallacy goes something like the following.

Never delay consequences with kids. If you do, you'll lose the teachable moment, and your child won't learn a thing.

What a load of barnyard waste! I wonder how many cases of child abuse have occurred because parents had this myth resting on their shoulders.

Much of this hooey was originally based on lab research conducted on rats, mice, monkeys, and pigeons. Despite what some folks seem to believe, children are far more intelligent than rats, mice, monkeys, and pigeons. The best way of proving this to yourself is by doing a little experiment:

• *Make your child a promise.*

Go ahead. Promise your child something that you know they really want. Maybe it's a trip to the "golden arches." Maybe it's a new toy. Maybe it's a cookie.

- *Tell them that you'll fulfill your promise later that day...or maybe the next.*
  Don't say another word about your promise.

- *See if they forget.*
  If a child is capable of remembering a promise, they are surely capable of remembering their misbehavior and hearing you say, "I'm going to do something about this later."

- *Of course, always fulfill the promises you make.*
  I put this part in to avoid getting nasty letters from folks who may misinterpret me as saying that we should make promises and not keep them.

The key purpose of this little experiment is to help people see... first hand...the following:

If a child can remember a promise, they can remember misbehaving and hearing you say, "I'm going to do something about that later."

Now let's see what transpired between me and my suddenly sassy employee. Cass had worked for me for almost ten years. (Of course, I've changed her name to avoid any subsequent sassiness.) Anyway, she'd been a wonderful and loyal employee for most of that time. Unfortunately, she began to feel more and more dissatisfied with her life. She perceived her job as boring... which I'm sure it was at times...and she wanted to do something that challenged her more and paid more pesos.

There was just one problem: She lacked the skills and education required for advancement within our company. Instead of developing these qualifications, she became mired in boredom and unhappiness. Personal calls to her friends during work hours were her way of making it through the day. She was a good person who was doing a really horrible job. Despite my attempts to help her develop additional skills, or to become happier in her current spot, she became more and more resentful and rebellious.

Does this sound like any children you know?

Then it happened...the straw that broke the camel's back. "This is stupid! You can't tell me what to do!"

I couldn't believe my ears! Did she really say that?

Making sure that I understood her point of view, she repeated herself, "This is stupid! You can't tell me what to do!"

As the shock wore off, my anger revved up. On the verge of letting loose and chewing her head off, I remembered that woman in my audience...that one who asked, "How does my friend do it when her kid says, 'You can't tell me what to do!'"

I also remembered the answer I provided, "When you can't think of what to do...or you're too angry to think straight, delay the consequence."

Then I thought, "If Mom and Dad raised me with any integrity at all, I'd better practice what I preach...right here and now!"

Bolting out of Cass's cubicle, I managed to mutter, "I'll talk with you about this tomorrow...I'm too angry to think straight."

The next day, I was far better prepared to lock in the empathy. She was calmer, too. There she sat in my office, sheepishly studying the carpet under her chair.

"I can't tell you how sad all of this makes me," I began, "I'm still having a hard time believing what happened yesterday."

Still studying the floor, she agreed, "I know, I know. I'm sorry."

"You haven't been happy here for months," I continued, "and I've had to talk with you a number of times."

With tears in her eyes, she mumbled, "I guess I'm fired?"

All I could manage was a sincerely sad, "Uh…yeah."

As she walked out of my office, I offered a handshake. She hugged me instead.

I drove home that afternoon truly astounded by the tremendous power of empathy…and sincerely thankful that I hadn't screamed, "You're fired!" the day before. As the years have passed, Cass has visited often…without any of the sass. From time to time, someone in my office will shout, "Hey! Cass's car is in the parking lot!" Then we'll all giggle and laugh with her about the "old days" and all of the shenanigans her kids are pulling. During every one of these visits, my heart feels glad and thankful.

Although all situations handled with empathy don't always turn out so nicely, we can always hold our heads high, knowing that we've treated our kids…and the adults around us…with great dignity and respect. Although we can't control how people will react, we can control how we do. When I lay my head down for the very last time, and they make a headstone for my grave, I hope they can honestly inscribe:

HERE LAYS AN IMPERFECT GUY WHO DID HIS BEST TO SHOW OTHERS HE CARED.

Applying empathy allows us the wonderfully comforting ability to look in the mirror each day and feel proud that we've done our best to bring the best out of others. It also ups the odds that our children will come to view mistakes as learning opportunities rather than calamities.

Although all situations handled with empathy don't always turn out so nicely, we can always hold our heads high, knowing that we've treated our kids…and the adults around us…with great dignity and respect.

Shirley wasn't lucky enough to grow up in this sort of home. Although her parents loved her very, very much, they weren't fond of foul-ups. Every day, they got out of bed with the very same thought, "Today we'd better make sure that our little Shirley doesn't blow it. And, if she does, we'd better make sure that she knows how upset it makes us."

Knowing Shirley's family very well, it's clear that this sort of thinking wasn't something new. From all accounts, it started hundreds of years earlier across the big pond. High in the Carpathian Mountains of Eastern Europe, Shirley's distant ancestors worried like crazy that their kids might blunder. Her ancestors in England fretted that theirs would spill the tea. When these wonderful yet worrying families collided in the new world, they married...and passed down centuries of tradition...and lots of worrying about mistakes. Their family motto read:

It's far better to bite your nails now than wish you had later.

Hundreds of years of practice makes perfect! With the greatest of ease, Shirley's parents consistently showed her how upset they were when she goofed:

- They were really mad when she left her tricycle in the rain.
- Things were just horrible when she didn't eat her beets.
- It was awful when she spilled her milk.
- How dreadful it was when she lost her mittens.
- How angry they got when she burned the dinner rolls.

By the time Shirley was a young adult, she feared mistakes so badly that she made a conscious decision to avoid them at all costs. This meant never making a decision, never taking a risk, and never trying anything new. By the time she neared her thirtieth birthday, depression and anxiety clouded every waking moment...and relentlessly visited her in her dreams. With mistakes being horrible things, it was clear to her that the world was a very threatening place...a place to be avoided as often as possible.

It's tempting to contemplate how much different Shirley's life would have been if her parents had replaced their anger with empathy. Would she have viewed herself with far greater respect? Would she have experienced far greater joy?

Shirley's parents weren't to blame. They were simply living out life scripts placed in motion centuries earlier. In both of their families, parents got really upset and angry when their kids made mistakes. Since they were raised that way, they automatically parented that way. And...so did Shirley.

Not long after her fortieth birthday, Shirley decided to change. She was tired of being worried, tired of feeling angry, tired of being sad, and tired of being mad at her children and husband. She was downright tired! Guided by a wonderful therapist, she began to see how her upbringing influenced how she viewed the world. She also began to make some little mistakes. How hard it must have been at first! How scary it must have been to take those little risks...and to see that the sky doesn't fall when you goof!

Shirley is a very real and very special person. Why do I know her and her family so well? I belong to the clan. Shirley is my mom. As she grew and learned self-confidence, so did I. Watching her struggle with her childhood, and watching her become generally enthusiastic and happy, has shaped my life beyond comprehension. From her example, I've learned that it's far better to make mistakes and live life than to sit around biting your nails. I've also learned that it's never too late to learn and grow. As you can probably guess, I love my mom!

It's far better to make mistakes and live life than to sit around biting your nails.

CHAPTER FIVE

No Problems…
Just Solutions

Raise The Most Creative Problem-Solvers in Town!

Mr. and Mrs. Glass dreamed for years of buying and renovating a historic home. As they stopped at the end of the rough cobbled street, their hearts leaped with joy as they gazed at it. There it was, a lace-trimmed Victorian, peeking out from behind decades of overgrown flora. "That's the one! It's perfect!" The deal was sealed and the house was theirs. It wasn't long before they realized that the only thing more crooked than the previous owner was the house. Their dreams seemed shattered, particularly after they hired Clyde the contractor.

"Can't be done" were Clyde's three favorite words.

"You got major cracks in this foundation, and you're asking if I can shore it up? Can't be done."

"These walls aren't plumb. You want these square cabinets in them un-square holes? Can't be done."

"I can't help it if the electrician walked off the job. Can't find another this week. Just can't be done."

"These wider tubs will never fit through the bathroom doors. Can't be done."

On the verge of cracking, the Glasses gave Clyde the boot. Tony and his crew showed up early the next day. "Can you do anything about this foundation?" asked Mr. Glass.

"No problem," Tony replied. "I'm not sure how we'll truss it up, but we'll look at some options and see which looks best."

"Yeah but, we know these walls aren't plumb," Mr. Glass interrupted. "How are you going to get these cabinets to fit?"

"No problem," Tony assured. "It looks like we'll need to cover the gaps with some decorative molding."

"Yeah but I bet you don't do electrical work," Mrs. Glass countered.

"No I don't," Tony admitted, "but I'll have no problem finding somebody really quick."

"Yeah but how will you get these bathtubs to fit through the bathroom doors?" both of the Glasses probed.

Tony chuckled, "We can't...but that's no problem. We can either take them through the windows or cut the doorways larger and repair them afterwards."

As Tony and his crew drove away, the Glasses thought, "No problem. No problem? Talk is cheap. We'll believe it when we see it!"

Mr. Munster of Munster Construction Company knew Tony was up to the job. Years ago, he'd taken a lot of grief for promoting him to superintendent. At that time, he was younger than most of the other employees, his framing and finish skills were green, and he'd never managed a crew. Mr. Munster saw something in Tony that was far more important and rare...the willingness and ability to confront and solve problems of all types. As an employer struggling to hire the best and the brightest, Mr. Munster soon learned that having skills is no substitute for general common sense and the willingness to consider a wide range of possible solutions to every challenge. Those with this ability quickly develop the unique skills required for each job. Those without it give up before they have a chance to use the skills they possess.

"Problem jobs" were Tony's favorite jobs, and "No problem" was his favorite saying. It wasn't long before the Glasses realized that Tony and Clyde were about as different as night and day. Where Clyde saw hassles and headaches, Tony saw potential and promise. Where Clyde perceived the impossible, Tony perceived the possible. Their foundation problems were fixed, their cabinets looked cool, their tubs were tucked neatly into place, and the wiring worked. Mr. and Mrs. Glass ended up with very little cash but plenty of appreciation for those who see solutions rather than problems.

Only those who know how to entertain and analyze unique solutions to unpredictable circumstances have what it takes to succeed.

Our great country won't be great for much longer if we don't begin to raise more young people with skills like Tony's. Over the past three decades, employers have seen a precipitous decline in the number of employees who possess flexible and creative problem-solving skills. Although many are very bright and have plenty of facts crammed into their heads, they act like fish out of water when unexpected challenges arise. When was the last time your job...or your life…ran smoothly according to a predictable, logical script? Only those who know how to entertain and analyze unique solutions to unpredictable circumstances have what it takes to succeed.

So, what do I mean by "problem-solving skills"? Folks who have them know how to:

- LISTEN and gather enough information to correctly identify the problem
- BRAINSTORM a list of potential solutions

- PREDICT the likely consequences of implementing each solution
- EXPERIMENT with the solution that seems best
- LEARN from the results and keep experimenting until the problem is solved

Will we be fortunate enough to have leaders with the guts and creativity to deal successfully with unpredictability and chaos?

Our country and the freedoms we enjoy are dependent upon future generations possessing creative problem-solving skills. Who will be the leaders of industry and government? Will it be those with lots of knowledge and very little wisdom? Will it be those who depend on events operating in predictable, orderly ways? Or will we be fortunate enough to have leaders with the guts and creativity to deal successfully with unpredictability and chaos?

I'm frequently asked, "Why are we seeing so many young people who lack these skills?" Listed below are just a few of the reasons:

- Parents are involving their children less and less in daily tasks requiring problem-solving. These include chores, basic home and vehicle maintenance, meal preparation, etc.
- As a result, kids are seeing fewer examples of adults grappling with problems and developing creative solutions.
- Children are also spending far more time being entertained by nifty gadgets than playing and working in creative ways.
- The problem-solving models portrayed on television have become progressively more dysfunctional.
- Many parents simply tell their kids what to do...instead of helping them learn how to think through their problems.
- Other parents simply do everything for their kids...instead of expecting them to struggle with problems and develop solutions.

- Responding to societal and governmental pressures, many schools are now spending most of their time teaching facts…and less time teaching how to creatively apply such facts to real-life problems.

It's not all gloom and doom! Sure, we're seeing these problems, but that's all they are…problems. Wouldn't it be ironic if…in this chapter on the importance of problem-solving…we decided that it was best to give up and admit defeat? With some help from the five E's of Love and Logic, we have the tools to give our kids a grand advantage in this area. In the process, we give our country the gift of future leaders who've got what it takes to preserve the liberties we enjoy.

Example

Little Jimmy and his brothers were lucky little kids. Since their parents didn't have two nickels to rub together, they had to pull together as a family to survive. When the car broke, they huddled around their father, Frank, as he figured out what went wrong. When he rode the bus to the wrecking yard, they sat right next to him. When he bought a used replacement part, they helped him carry it home. When he repaired the car, they stayed nearby, handing him the right tools.

Ray and his brothers weren't so lucky. Since their parents had enough money to buy what they needed, they rarely had an opportunity to help out. When the car wouldn't start, their dad called the mechanic, and they played with their hand-held video games.

Jimmy and his sibs were good at helping their mother, too! When she'd scraped together enough cash to buy paint for the kitchen, they grabbed their paint brushes and went to work. From watching her every move, they learned to get most of the paint on the walls instead of on the floor…and themselves. "Paint costs a lot of money," she'd remind. "That's why it's important to figure out how to hold your brush so that it doesn't drip off."

Ray and his siblings were soon bored with the professional house painters hired by their parents. Believe it or not, they wouldn't even let kids help! They just worked. Rather than watching paint dry, the boys escaped to the "family" room... where over 200 channels of high-definition cable TV were at their fingertips.

Summer vacation was a time of great excitement and joy in Jimmy's home. On the hottest days, they'd trek down to the South Platte River and skip stones across its surface. "You have to try a lot of different rocks to find ones that really skip," their pop would point out. "The big chunky round ones just go plop."

One year Jimmy and his brothers even found enough scrap wood and used nails to build a tree house. As they worked, they experimented. From this experimentation, they learned how to straighten bent nails so they don't re-bend when you whack them. From trial and error, they also learned that scrap wood tends to spit really easy unless you're careful about where you hammer the nails. If you put them too close to the end of the board, you'll end up with two or three boards instead!

Summer was super for Ray's tribe, too. The slide at Silly Willie's Water Park was awesome, the roller coaster at Thrill Village was sweet, and their new remote control cars were a blast. There was also plenty of uninterrupted time for playing hand-held video games and watching high-def cable in the "family" room.

It's not too tough to spot the pattern here. From which family will the most creative kids emerge? Which will be equipped with the most adaptive problem-solving skills? While growing up in Ray's family is exciting and fun, very little creativity and problem-solving is required. When problems come up, somebody else gets paid to solve them. Because of their life situation,

Jimmy's parents are unable to provide much entertainment... and they certainly don't have the cash to hire much help. As a result, the entire family has endless opportunities to learn.

As we reflect on these two families, it's important to point out that there's nothing wrong with hiring a mechanic...or a house painter! Some limited time playing appropriate video games and watching appropriate TV shows won't cause brain damage. Trips to amusement parks can be awesome. Remote control toys really are fun! While there's nothing inherently wrong with these wonderful privileges, they're frequently over-used in too many families. As a result, some very unfortunate things begin to happen:

- Kids begin to expect life to be fun and entertaining all of the time.
- They come to believe that it is someone else's job to make sure that they never get bored.
- As a result, they often refuse to do difficult things...or they give up when the task becomes a bit dull.
- Not surprisingly, they find it extremely difficult to stay focused in school, particularly when their teacher is less entertaining than their video games at home.
- They lack critical opportunities to struggle with difficulties, achieve success, and feel great about their accomplishment.
- They miss out on participation in family activities where they see problem-solving skills modeled by adults.

Let's consider this final concern. As you know by now, the first "E" of Love and Logic stands for Example. If children aren't seeing the special adults in their lives grappling with problems, gathering helpful information, developing creative solutions, and learning through trial and error, how will they ever learn to do the same? The world is filled with well-meaning parents like Ray's. In an attempt to give their kids the best, they're actually depriving them of critical learning opportunities. By creating a home where children are never required to help, they're creating kids who don't know how to help.

If children aren't seeing the special adults in their lives grappling with problems, how will they ever learn to do the same?

Jimmy grew up to be someone near and dear to the hearts of millions. His creative solutions to complex parenting and educational problems have been improving lives around the world for the past forty years. Jimmy grew up to be my father, Jim Fay. For those of you new to Love and Logic, Jimmy and his good friend Foster W. Cline, M.D. founded the Love and Logic Institute. Like so many people who've changed the world, both of them grew up in families where the children were heavily involved in the often mundane duties required to keep a household afloat. By working alongside their parents, and watching their example, they developed a basic mental template for problem-solving. Once this template sears itself into the brain, it remains a permanent guide for solving problems of all kinds, ranging from the rather simple (e.g., how to straighten bent nails) to the very complex (e.g., how to maintain positive relationships with demanding customers and bosses).

One of my earliest memories involves helping my father plaster the basement walls of our home. If you've ever raised kids, you know what it means to have a three- or four-year-old "help." Bless his heart! Instead of blowing his top, he bit his tongue and plodded along. Since he wasn't a professional plasterer, this provided a wonderful opportunity for me to see some good old-fashioned problem-solving. It also gave me a great chance to hear my pop ponder possible solutions.

When gravity took over and the plaster started running down the wall, he wondered out loud, "Why won't this stay put?

Maybe it's too runny. Maybe if I mix in a little more powder. Maybe it'll be thick enough to stay on until it dries. Let's see."

We were extremely lucky as children. Since we lived in a very isolated and mountainous area, there were only two television channels to choose from. Both had more static than picture. In fact, I was probably sixteen years old before I learned that it didn't really snow on Gilligan's Island. The up-side was that my sisters and I spent far more time playing creatively and helping our parents than vegetating in front of the tube.

We were fortunate for another reason. Our parents had very little money. Since Mom stayed home with us…and Dad was a school teacher…they didn't have the cash required to pay someone to fix the car, repair the plumbing, replace broken septic lines, etc. Therefore, there were always plenty of opportunities for us to see…and hear…our parents struggling through problems.

We can model great problem-solving by thinking out loud…and allowing our kids to overhear it.

By his very nature, my father has always been a loud thinker. Some folks are quiet thinkers, but his thoughts have volume. Yep, when he's tackling a problem, his lips move and words pop out. Fortunately, the words he uses are rated "G"! As we were growing up, those words also gave us lots of opportunities to hear how good problem-solvers think. How do we model good problem-solving when much of the process is something that goes on inside of our heads? Simply by allowing our kids to overhear the following:

- "What's going wrong here? What's the problem?"
- "What could I try to solve this problem?"
- "What seems to be the best solution so far? How would that work for me?"

- "I'm starting to get pretty frustrated with this. I better take a break and get some more information."
- "Where can I learn more about solving this problem? Who can give me advice on this? I wonder if there are any books I could read. Maybe there's some good information on the internet?"
- "I think I'll try doing _____."
- "That didn't work out so well...but that's good information. What else might I try?"

Are your kids spending all of their time being entertained, or are they getting a chance to learn? Are they getting enough opportunities to participate in family chores and family problem-solving, or are they spending most of their time being entertained by exciting gadgets? Are they seeing your example as you tackle challenges and work through them, or are they coming to believe that you just hire others to solve problems? Are they receiving the gift of hearing you think your way through the process, or are you keeping all of this great cogitation to yourself? If you're worried that your kids aren't seeing enough examples of good problem-solving, it's never too late to get started!

Expectation
At my seminars, I'm often asked, "What's the most important thing we must achieve as parents?"

After years of studying really successful...and not-so-successful...parents, I've settled on a single, consistent answer, "Raise children who don't need us."

To some folks this makes total sense. They nod their heads and smile in response. To others it widens their eyes in shock. From their mouths come audible gasps of horror. To some, raising independent, self-reliant kids is second nature. To others, it's downright threatening.

The most important thing we must achieve as parents is to raise children who don't need us.

Some parents are like Gloria. Growing up, she felt loved, secure, and competent. As a result, she finds it quite natural to raise kids who know how to solve problems. Although she experiences a slight twinge of loss each time they became more independent, she jumps for joy knowing that they're well on their way to becoming healthy, responsible adults! Knowing that they need her less every day doesn't frighten her. Seeing them get angry at her doesn't scare her either. Why? Simply because she isn't reliant on them for meeting her need to be needed.

Folks like Gloria aren't uncomfortable allowing their kids to struggle with the problems they encounter. When their tots complain, "Monsters are under my bed!" the Glorias of the world find it easy to hug them and reply, "Well, sweetie...what do you think you can do? Would it be best for you to sleep with your light on or learn those monsters' names and make friends with them? I know you'll figure something out. See you in the morning."

When their teenagers complain, "I lost my cell phone!" Gloria-like parents find it easy to inquire, "I bet that feel's horrible. Have you given any thought to how you are going to pay for a replacement?"

Other parents are like Kurt...who grew up feeling unloved, insecure, and generally incompetent. He's got a heart full of hurt. The only time this hurt seems to go away is when others are relying on him to solve their problems. The only time he really feels good about himself is when he's playing superhero, rescuing his children from the unfair world. Each time his children grow a bit more independent, anxiety...panic...rips through his body. His subconscious mind screams, "Who will I rescue? My kids are getting far too competent. I'd better nip that in the bud!" Without awareness, he stifles their growth, ensuring the continued security of his superhero status.

The Kurts of the world find it terrifying to sit back and allow their kids to solve the problems they encounter. When their tots complain, "Monsters are under my bed!" their superhero instincts kick in. "That's horrible," they reply. "You'll be safe sleeping with Mommy and Daddy."

When their teens complain, "I lost my cell phone!" Kurt-like parents rush to their aid, "Well, ok. I'll buy you another...but you need to be more responsible!"

If reading about Gloria and Kurt makes you hate this book, it probably means that I've touched a truth in your life that you're not ready to confront. If it leaves you feeling a sense of guilt or remorse, it's important to remember that it's never too late to help your kids by helping yourself. The healthier we become, the easier it is to raise healthy, responsible kids.

It's never too late to help your kids
by helping yourself.
The healthier we become, the easier it is
to raise healthy, responsible kids.

The Second "E" of Love and Logic stands for Expectation. It's clear to see which of these parents finds it easiest to set and enforce high ones! For Gloria, it's a breeze. When her kids spout silly things like, "I hate you!" or "You don't care!" she finds it easy to remain firm. Instead of backing down, she calmly repeats, "I love you too much to argue. I know you can solve this problem. If you'd like some ideas, just let me know."

Sticking to limits and expectations is just too scary for Kurt. Because he depends so heavily on his children to meet his needs, it feels like the end of the world when they complain about him being mean. When he hears, "I hate you!" or "You don't care!"

terror strikes his heart. Down deep he worries, "If they're unhappy with me, they might find somebody else to be their hero!"

Do Kurt's children know his Achilles' heal? Do they know exactly what to say in order to make him back down and do their bidding? When they become employees some day, what are the odds that their bosses will appreciate this sort of manipulative behavior?

As Gloria's kids grow, there'll be times when they view her as being too strict, too old-fashioned and just plain "lame"! That's the price we pay for setting high expectations and expecting our kids to own and solve their problems. It's also the price we pay for raising great employees and great citizens. Ironically, parents who're willing to pay the piper when their children are young, end up enjoying far happier and more respectful kids. Why? All people are born with a very strong drive to gain mastery over the challenges present in their lives...and to feel independent. Parents who operate in ways that support this innate drive enjoy the best long-term relationships with their kids. Down deep, their children appreciate the fact that they were expected to own and solve their problems. As adults, it's not unusual to hear them say:

When I was growing up, my parents loved me enough to expect the very best from me. They loved me enough to expect me to behave, and they loved me enough to show me how to be a successful adult.

Unlike Gloria, Kurt's taking the "credit-card" approach to raising kids. Instead of paying the price early on, he's decided to defer payment by trying to make his youngsters happy all of the time. Like many politicians, superhero Kurt wants his children's votes too badly to stand for anything unpopular. As a result, it's not unusual for the Kurts of the world to enjoy short-term friendships with their kids.

**There will be times when our kids view us
as being too strict, too old-fashioned and just plain
"lame"! That's the price we pay for raising
great employees and great citizens.**

Sadly, children always grow to resent parents who are friends
instead of parents. Friend-like parents fail to establish the sorts of
expectations that enable children to develop problem-solving skills
and pride. As these children grow, so do their feelings of hostile-
dependency toward the adults in their lives who've thwarted their
growth. Down deep, they understand that these people hampered
their ability to become independent and self-respecting adults.
That's why they often complain to their therapists:

> *My parents didn't even care enough to expect me to behave.
> All they ever did was give me stuff and try to be my buddy. No
> wonder my life is such a train wreck!*

From over thirty years of research, we've seen what happens
when kids grow up with parents like Gloria...and what happens
when they grow up with parents like Kurt. We've also observed
what takes place when they grow up with both of these parenting styles in the same home.

What's the result when one parent tries to set reasonably high
expectations for problem-solving...while the other spends most
of their time "rescuing" the kids from these expectations? If
you're a Gloria...and your spouse (or ex-spouse) is a Kurt, what
can you do to up the odds that your kids will grow up with the
gift of good problem-solving? To answer these questions, let's
consider the case of Erin and Eddie.

Their marriage was relatively friction-free until the day their
little Wanda crawled over to the curtains and gave them a good,
solid yank. "Uh oh!" sang Eddie, as he gently picked her up and

placed her in her bassinette. "You can come out as soon as you can act sweet."

"Eddie!" Erin scolded as she rescued Wanda, "You're just upsetting her by doing that!"

A bit more tension crept into the marriage when two-year old Wanda whined, "Mommy! Daddy! I want to sleep with you!"

With a loving hug and empathy in his voice, Eddie replied, "Oh…I can understand wanting to do that. You need to stay in your room. Do you want your light on or off?"

"Eddie!" Erin chastised, "can't you see that she's really scared?"

Casting a pensive look her mother's way, Wanda wailed, "I'm scared! I want to sleep with you!"

"That's ok," Mother comforted. "You can sleep with Mommy and Daddy."

Things weren't any better four years later…

"Daddy, I can't tie my shoes! It's too hard!"

"Oh, sweetie," he replied with love, "I know you can do it. I've seen you tie them before. You are such a big girl!"

"Eddie!" Erin erupted as she bent to tie Wanda's laces. "Didn't you hear her? Why do you expect her to do things she can't do?"

By this time, Wanda had perfected the tactic of tossing a woeful look her mother's way…then sitting back and watching the sparks fly. There was never any doubt in her young mind that Mom would come to the rescue…while simultaneously shredding Daddy's ego with the voracity of a wood chipper whipping through freshly cut saplings.

From her throne, Queen Wanda the Terrible controlled her tiny kingdom with the greatest of ease! Like all dictators, though, she hungered for more. The next step toward world domination required that she conquer Lincoln Heights Elementary School. By tossing her signature "helpless-look-full-o-woe" her mother's way, she was quite certain that mommy dearest would squash those mean and insensitive school people like grapes in a wine press.

"It's so horrible. I can't even talk about it!" Wanda sniffled.

"What's wrong?" Erin pleaded.

Strategically applying the "look," Wanda moaned, "My teacher never helps me. She doesn't even care. She never explains anything."

"That's it!" Erin raged. "I've had it with that school!"

For a brief moment, Eddie thought he saw Wanda's lips curl into an evil smile. Sighing, he thought, "*%&#$@! Here we go again!"

> **Kids grow to respect parents who give them the most skills for being successful in life. They grow to resent parents who are too busy being their friends to give them these skills.**

While Wanda is well on her way to becoming the type of whiney, manipulative employee bosses dread, Eddie still has the power to divert this runaway train by giving her a little taste of what it takes to become a healthy adult. This can only happen if he's willing to be the bad guy in the short term. If he is, Wanda will get a dose of healthy parenting…even if her mother never changes her ways. From over three decades of work with families like Wanda's, we've learned that this little dose can go a long way toward helping kids eventually grow into healthy adults. In fact, there's a darn good chance that Wanda will turn out wonderful if she gets enough high-expectation behavior from her daddy.

Unfortunately, parents like Eddie often give up instead of giving this gift. Because they've been mowed down so many times, they begin to reason, "It's no use. Why try? What good does it do if every time I try to discipline the kids I get hammered? I'm tired of being the bad guy!"

If you're a parent like Eddie don't give up! There's good news! Although your kids will probably view you as a villain in the short term, they will more than likely grow to respect and love you in the long term. That is…if you are willing to hold your ground in a loving way.

That's exactly what Eddie's best friend told him, "When our kids were young, my wife and I used to argue all of the time about how we were raising them. I'm a lot stricter than she is… and I guess she's just a lot more nurturing that I am. Then we learned at our Love and Logic class that kids can turn out ok… even if their parents don't always agree on discipline."

"They can?" Eddie asked.

"Yeah," his buddy replied, "we learned that it's ok to handle the kids differently just as long as you don't fight about it in front of them…or make each other look bad. In the long run, the kids will come to respect the parent who gave them the most skills for being successful in life."

A spark of hope ignited in Eddie's heart. "Do you really think that's true? What do your kids think now?"

"Now that they're older," his friend answered, "they still treat their mom like a doormat…but they treat me really good."

"So there's hope?" Eddie asked.

Nodding, his friend replied, "Yep! The best thing we ever did for our kids…and our marriage…was to agree that it's okay for us to have different parenting styles."

"So how did you do it?" Eddie asked.

"When my wife said something to the kids, "He continued, "I tried to stay out of it…even when I thought what she was doing was sort of dumb. Then she did her best to do the same. We both did our best to avoid saying anything to put each other down in front of the kids."

"Well," Eddie countered, "didn't the kids try to manipulate you against each other?"

Chuckling, his friend replied, "Oh, yes! They tried, but it didn't work for them. When they'd complain, 'Mom lets us do that!' I'd just smile and say, 'Well...aren't you lucky to have such a nice mom! I don't let you.'"

"Well," Eddie continued to query, "what happened when they complained to your wife about you being too strict?"

"Most times she just smiled and said something like, 'You're so lucky to have a strict dad! Someday when you have a strict boss, you'll know how to handle him.'"

Eddie had one more question for his friend: "Where do we sign up for that Love and Logic class?"

Yes! It's true! Kids really can turn out ok...even when their parents disagree about how to raise them. Listed below are some quick tips for giving your kids the gift of a high-expectation parent when your spouse (or ex spouse) isn't:

Create a personal parenting mission statement.
Folks are more successful when they identify their long-term goals and take the time to write them down in the form of a parenting mission statement. Here's a brief example:

> *As I raise these kids of mine, my primary goal is to create respectful, responsible, humble and hardworking adults. To this end, I will show them great love while setting and enforcing firm limits. I'll also resist the urge to make them dependent upon me by rescuing them from the struggles they will face. Because I'm focused on what's best for them in the long run, I won't be afraid to stay firm...even if they complain or try to manipulate me. I will also remember that doing the right thing for my kids is not always going to be popular with the other adults around me. Since I believe so strongly in what I am doing, I will forever remind myself that it's okay to be the bad guy in the short term if this means raising great people in the long term.*

When the going gets tough in the short term…when we feel pressured to back down…having a clearly articulated mission helps us hold firm. Like a tree with strong roots, we're far more likely to remain upright during the inevitable storms of life.

Don't waste time trying to change your spouse.
Wise people don't waste precious time and energy trying to control others. As a result, they find it far easier to control themselves

Don't undermine your spouse (or ex-spouse).
This always backfires!

Agree to be different.
Arguing and fighting over having different styles does far more damage to the kids than having different styles.

Review your mission statement at least once a week.
This will help you remain more confident and consistent.

Be prepared to be the "bad guy."
While we all want our kids to view us as heroes, this is more about our own needs and desires than what's best for them.

Education

There are two types of parents who operate like helicopters on high-stakes search and rescue missions. Some are like Kurt. They rescue their kids from high expectations in desperate attempts to meet their own need to be needed. Kurt-like parents are rarely open to change. Because their behavior is driven by deep-seated pathological needs, they have tremendous difficulty believing that they are doing anything wrong. Instead, they perceive the rest of the world as being "mean" or "insensitive" to their child's needs. While it's not impossible for spouses of such parents to hold the line and give their kids the gift of problem-solving, it's a long and difficult road.

Most hovering types are more like Erin. Instead of rescuing because of deep-seated needs, they do so because they've never learned a better way....and they've yet to experience enough pain and exhaustion from their super-hero-like behavior. When these parents encounter the right combination of parental angst AND practical ideas, they quickly learn that there's a far more satisfying and effective way to parent. Their anguish and exhaustion provide the motivation. Love and Logic provides the education!

As I walked down the concourse at McCarren International Airport, I wondered, "What type of parent would hire me to travel all the way from Denver...and pay my consulting fee... out of her own pocket...to share the message of Love and Logic with others in her community?"

Waiting for my luggage at the baggage claim, I continued to daydream. It was all so surreal...the sound of slot machines, fight announcements, and the red siren on top of the luggage carousel. (Yes! For those of you who've never been to Vegas, there really are slot machines in the airport.) "Las Vegas"...I thought. "Brought to Vegas to teach Love and Logic...by a mom who just decided that it would be a nice gift to give her neighbors. She seemed like a nice lady over the phone...I wonder if they use Love and Logic in casinos? I doubt it...They could have slot machines that say, 'How sad, what a bummer!' as they gobble your cash."

"Dr. Fay? Is that you? Dr. Fay?"

Roused from my daydream, I saw her smiling face and outstretched hand. "Hello! Dr. Fay. I'm Erin. It's so nice to meet you in person. We've been looking forward to your visit!"

As we drove from the airport...and the glitz and glamour of the Strip, she described how she became so passionate about Love and Logic. "I was at my wits end! I was the quintessential hovering, rescuing helicopter parent. I devoted every last erg of energy to making sure that our daughter Wanda was never unnecessarily challenged, upset or even slightly inconvenienced. Any time she had a problem, I rushed to the rescue! When my husband tried to say 'no' to her, I said 'yes'...and then I really made him pay. Any time she got a bad grade at school, I rushed down to her school and demanded that they give her a second chance...and then a third one. The older she got, the more problems she needed me to solve. I was a mess...and so was my marriage!"

"So," I asked, "what changed your ways?"

"It wasn't Love and Logic," she smiled. "At least at first it wasn't. I thought the Love and Logic class Eddie and I took made no sense at all. I think the reason I didn't like it was because he did! I wasn't quite ready to believe that my old way of doing things was actually creating a needy, whiney, manipulative kid."

"So," I joked, "the reason you hired me is because you think Love and Logic stinks?"

"No!" she smiled. "Of course not! It's the best thing that ever happened to me. It's just that I wasn't ready for it...well...I wasn't ready until two things happened. First, I started seeing how good it was working for Eddie. That really galled me!"

"What was the second thing?" I inquired.

"It was when Wanda's fourth grade teacher pulled me aside one morning and said, 'Erin, I think that Wanda is old enough to find her own classroom this year. There's no need to lead her there each morning."

"Oh, I bet that made you mad!"

She nodded, "At first it really did, but then I started thinking about it. For some reason, it made more sense coming from this teacher than it did coming from my husband. Or…maybe I was just ready to hear the truth."

"So," I asked, "this really changed things for you?"

"Oh, yes! It was like I suddenly realized, 'I don't have to sit across the street from the school with my binoculars trained on the playground anymore!'"

I gasped, "What? Surely you didn't—"

"Oh, yes," Erin interrupted. "I used to sit there every day during Wanda's recess, making sure that she never got picked on. She'd been crying every day after school about being called names…and not having any friends to play with…so I decided to take matters into my own hands and make sure everything went smoothly for her. I cringe admitting that! That's why you're here! I want other parents at our school to hear how important it is to empower their kids to own and solve their problems… rather than cripple them by forever racing to the rescue."

"I guess that strong-willed adults," I replied, "have to learn their most important lessons the same way as strong-willed children."

"You bet!" she laughed. "By making lots of mistakes and experiencing the consequences!"

As we talked, Erin described how she began to take a very different approach with wonderful Wanda. "Whenever she'd complain about being picked on at school, or having a mean teacher, or having a mean dad, or anything else, I'd replace rescuing with those five steps you teach…those steps for guiding kids to own and solve their problems."

"That must have been tough!" I replied.

"At first it was," she admitted. "But then I got addicted. I couldn't believe what a weight it took off of my shoulders! It was so freeing!"

As Erin described her personal journey as a recovering Helicopter parent, she described the five steps discussed on pages 47 through 50:

- Provide a strong and sincere dose of empathy.
- Ask your child, "What do you think you are going to do?"
- When your child says, "I don't know," ask, "Would you like to hear some ideas?"
- Give your child two or three options. After each ask, "How will that work for you?"
- Resist the urge to tell your child which solution to use.

The first time she applied this process was one afternoon when Wanda pouted her way into the house after school. "Nobody likes me! Nobody wants to be my friend. They just call me 'Weird Wanda.' I wish I was never born!"

Resisting the urge to call the parents of these children, Erin delivered a warm dollop of empathy instead. "Oh, honey, that's got to really hurt your feelings."

Wanda agreed, "Yeah, Mom. They're so mean. And my teachers don't even do anything!"

Erin eased into step two, "What do you think you're going to do?"

With eyeballs the size of Frisbees, Wanda whined, "I'm doing something! I'm telling you!"

Erin rolled on to step three, "Would you like to hear some ideas?"

Wanda wasn't happy about her mother's new parenting prowess, "What am I supposed to do? It's not my fault those kids are such jerks!"

Now it was time for step four, "Some kids decide to feel sorry for themselves. How would that work for you?"

Wanda's eyes grew even wilder, "That's crazy, Mom!"

"Well, honey, some kids decide to trick those other kids into thinking that they're too cool to be bothered by those silly names. How would that work?"

Wanda's curiosity was piqued, "What do you mean?"

"Some kids just say something silly like, 'Thanks for the information' or 'I know.'"

Wanda grumbled, "That won't work!"

Now it was time for the fifth and final step, "Well, honey, good luck. Let me know how this works out for you. If you would like any other ideas, come and ask."

Dejected and depressed, Erin went into her bedroom, threw herself on the bed, and wept. "That went well!" she thought with stinging sarcasm, "What do I do now?"

The next afternoon, at the depth of her despair, a tiny ray of hope glimmered through the gloom and doom. As Wanda tossed her backpack on the couch, she proudly proclaimed, "It was hilarious!"

"What was so funny?" Erin prodded.

"That Rachel Jenkins...you know that skinny girl that always wears boy's clothes? Well, she told me that I was weird."

"Why is that so funny?" Mother asked.

"Well," Wanda continued, "I just told her that it's true and that weirdness is contagious. Then she just laughed. She didn't even know what to say!"

At that precise moment Erin realized that there's no greater gift we can give our kids than the self-esteem associated with owning and solving their problems.

Experience

People often ask, "Is it ever too late? If my kid is a teen or adult, is it too late for them to learn these skills?"

My answer is always the same, "As long as you're still young enough to learn these techniques, it's never too late to use them with success on your kids!"

**As long as you're still young enough
to learn these techniques, it's never too late
to use them with success on your kids!**

Twenty-three-year-old Lex Leisureman lived at home with his loving father and evil stepmother. His stepmother, Lonnie, was wicked because she wanted him to do completely inappropriate things like help with the dishes, operate the vacuum cleaner, and pick up his dirty clothes. In fact she was so despicable that she actually had the gall to suggest that he either go back to school or get a job!

Lester, his dad, was a different story. The great thing about Dad was that he never placed too much undo pressure on his leisure-loving son. He always understood when Lex was having a bad day and spewed insults at him and his new wife. He always understood when Lex refused to help with the housework. "It's tough being a kid these days," he'd defend. "He's got so much on his mind."

There were no limits to father Lester's understanding! When Lex needed a few extra dollars to hang with his friends...or to buy a new stereo...or to pay a traffic ticket, Dad was always a real trooper. When wicked stepmom swooped in on her broom, and complained about Lex's fiscal faults, Dad was quick to excuse, "I don't know why you get so bent out of shape about me giving him a few dollars. It's not like we can't afford to help him out."

The fourth "E" of Love and Logic stands for Experience. As parents we can either provide experiences that allow our kids to develop maturity and good character...or we can protect them from such experiences. In America today, there exists an epidemic of parents who are so fearful of upsetting their youngsters...and of allowing them to experience any struggle...that they are willing to let them remain dependent upon them well into adulthood. As a result, our collective societal back is breaking under the weight of trying to support the massive numbers of young people who lack the skills and attitudes required to maintain gainful employment and to support the children they produce.

Our collective societal back is breaking under the weight of trying to support the massive numbers of young people who lack the skills and attitudes required to maintain gainful employment and to support the children they produce.

Love and Logic is an internship program for life. Parents who apply it make their homes operate as much like the real world as possible. As a result, their kids have plenty of safe opportunities to struggle with problems, make decisions, and experience the consequences of their decisions. When their children have a demanding teacher, these parents rejoice. They know that the struggle this teacher provides will give their child the experience necessary for working for demanding bosses. When their kids forget to do their chores, these parents hold their kids accountable by saying, "This is such a bummer. You forgot to do your chores, so I had to do them. Now I don't have the time and energy to drive you to your friends." They understand that kids who are taught to do their jobs without reminders become adults who know how to do the same! Because of this real-world focus, employers absolutely adore kids raised in Love and Logic homes!

Love and Logic is an internship program for life. Because of this real-world focus, employers absolutely adore kids raised in Love and Logic homes!

As Lex's twenty-fourth birthday loomed large on the horizon, his stepmom, Lonnie, was wondering whether his father was ever going to let him experience the real world. And she was livid about it. "Lester" she spouted, "it wouldn't be so bad if he was at least making some sort of an attempt to become a respectful and responsible human being, but all he does is lounge around and expect us to kiss his backside!"

The kettle continued to boil over, "I am sick and tired of waiting on him and having the both of you treat me like a doormat! I don't think I'm asking too much to be treated with some respect. I've had it...either he goes...or I do!"

Now the cards were on the table, and Lester looked like a deer in the headlights.

"I love you," she continued, "but I've had it!"

Two days later Lester was still in shock as he sat next to Lonnie in Dr. Couch's office. "I didn't know this was bothering you so much," he mumbled. "I mean, I knew that you were upset about it, but I had no idea you were this upset."

Lonnie bit her tongue, resisting the urge to list the hundreds of times she'd tried to get Lester to wake up and smell the coffee.

Leaning forward in her chair, Dr. Couch interrupted, "How much time and money would you like to waste with me over this issue?"

"What? Uh...well...none," Lester and Lonnie blurted in unison.

"Oh, that's good," Dr. Couch replied with a smile. "Some people want to spend years having me try to uncover their deep-seated emotional and marital problems. Others simply want some effective skills so that they can solve them on their own. It sounds like the two of you are the second type? Am I correct about that?"

Lester agreed, "Yeah, it's not like we're the Rockefellers or Bill Gates!"

Lonnie did, too. "That's for sure."

Dr. Couch continued, "Good...so let me make this really simple. Lex needs to be kicked out of the house in a loving way. I can teach you how to do this in four sessions or less. Are you still interested?"

Once again, Lester looked like Bambie, staring at the grill of a speeding Buick.

Feeling a twinge of compassion for the old guy, Lonnie stepped into the road, dragged him to safety, and replied, "We just need a little time to think about this. Can we give you a call and let you know?"

Three days later Lex lamented, "Dad, this sucks! It's like my phone fell in the toilet and now it doesn't work. These things are so cheap. I shoulda got that one that downloads tunes anyway. It's only like 200 bucks."

Lester lost it. "I just bought you that phone two weeks ago! How many times do I have to tell you to be more careful? Do you think that money grows on trees?"

Like usual, Lex had a perfectly reasonable explanation, "Dad! It's not like I did it on purpose. It was an accident. I put it in my front shirt pocket, and then…oh, I suppose you never make any mistakes. Besides, how am I supposed to get a hold of you if there's some sort of emergency? It's only 200 bucks. It's not like you can't afford it!"

Those two sentences rang in his head all night long… "It's only 200 bucks. It's not like you can't afford it…It's only 200 bucks. It's not like you can't afford it. It's only…"

The very next morning, a tearful Lester hugged his amazingly patient wife and said, "You've been right this whole time. I've created a monster!"

Over the next three weeks, the good doctor helped them understand why their son was so resentful, rebellious, and apathetic:

- Down deep, Lex was well aware that his father was standing in the way of his ability to grow competent and self-sufficient.
- With each passing day, Lex felt more frustrated and hostile about feeling so dependent upon his father.

- With each passing minute, Lex also felt more fearful and insecure about whether he was really capable of making his own way in the world.
- As a result of this dependency, fear, and depression, Lex found it safer to lounge around the house than to try bettering himself.

Lester also learned how to write a very special letter to his son:

Dear Lex:

I need to apologize. I am so sorry! I've been stealing from you for years.

I haven't taken anything like money...or any of your things. What I've stolen is your self-respect. I've also stood in the way of you becoming a man. I haven't done this on purpose. I did it because I love you very much. I really thought that I was doing the right thing by protecting you from the world. Now I realize that you need a chance to see that you have what it takes to make it in the world.

When you were just a little boy, you were afraid to learn how to swim. Because I worried that you might drown if you ever fell in a pond or a pool, I forced you to get in the water for your first lesson. You were so mad at me! That's until you learned how to float and paddle your way around the pool. Then you were so proud. On the way home from the pool, you smiled from ear to ear!

That's what I want for you now. That's why I'm expecting you to dive into adulthood by moving out and becoming completely self-supporting.

If you decide that you would like to continue your education by going to trade school or community college, you may live with us as long as you are doing your fair share of housework, are fun to be around, and are earning money to help us with utilities, food, and other miscellaneous expenses.

Let me know what you decide.

Love,

Dad.

Believe it or not, Lex was not impressed by Pop's carefully crafted letter! In fact, he blew a gasket, "Dad! How am I supposed to move out when I don't have any money? This is so unfair! You know how expensive things are these days!"

Lester was prepared to stand firm, "I know. Things are hard out there, but you can do it."

Lex went for the jugular. "You don't care. Ever since Lonnie came along, all you do is try to suck up to her. I know what this is all about. It's just her brainwashing you."

Dad replied, "Lex...I love you too much to argue about this."

Stomping into his room, Lex screamed, "You don't love me. If you loved me, you wouldn't be throwing me out in the street so that you could play house with that witch!"

Open heart surgery, performed with a rusty pocketknife and no anesthesia, would have felt better than the emotional dagger Lex plunged into his father's heart.

Lex emerged from his room lugging a duffle bag full of clothes and a "I-know-you'll-beg-me-to-stay-at-the-last-moment" look on his face. "We'll, I hope you're happy," he sneered, "I'm leaving."

Dad replied, "I love you. If you'd like to take a couple days and find a place to live first, that'd be okay."

Twisting the dagger a bit deeper, Lex replied, "That's ok. I know when I'm not wanted somewhere. Besides, I don't have to put up with this %$*#@&$ over at Mom's place. She isn't selfish. She'll let me hang out as long as I want."

As his son slammed the front door behind him, Lester felt lower than an earthworm. "Yep," he thought, "he'll just go over to his mom's. She'll let him do whatever he wants. Then the phone will start ringing off of the hook. First it'll be his mother, wanting to know why I'm so mean. Then it'll be her parents, chastising me for being too tough on their grandson. Then it'll be my sister, blasting me over the fact that I kicked my own flesh and blood into the street. Then my parents will call, just to let me know how disappointed they are in me."

When we do the right thing with challenging kids, there will be no shortage of folks who'll criticize us for being too strict, uncaring, or downright mean! In today's society, many loving yet misguided people believe that children should never have to encounter any stress or hardship. As a result, they absolutely freak out when someone close to them demonstrates some loving backbone with their children. Lester, like so many other parents trying to become more effective with their irresponsible children, became the family villain. As the calls began to roll in, Lester tried to remind himself that doing the right thing isn't always popular.

When we do the right thing with challenging kids, there will be no shortage of folks who'll criticize us for being too strict, uncaring, or downright mean!

He and his wife prayed long and hard that they'd done the right thing. As they did, they remembered some hopeful words uttered by Dr. Couch:

As our kids become mature adults, they come to realize which adults gave them the greatest shot at a life full of self-competence and joy. They also understand which adults stood in their way by enabling them to remain immature and unskilled. They come to respect and love those who expected them to grow...and they grow to resent those who didn't.

Empathy

Lester looked out the window just in time to see a shiny, near-new Ford Mustang rumble proudly into the driveway. It had been two months since Lex moved in with his mom, and it was clear that his change of venue was paying off quite nicely! Lester was filled with a strange combination of warmth...and massive irritation. It was great to see his son, but he thought, "Where the heck did he get the money to buy that?" Sarcastically, he mused, "What a great car for a kid living in the mountains of Colorado...ought to be able to drive that for two months out of the year!"

"How's it going?" Lex waved as he walked up the steps. "I was driving by and just thought I'd see what was going on. I'm real sorry about saying those mean things to you guys. I was just in a really bad place...ya know?"

As soon as Dad gazed into his son's baby blue eyes, time stood still. Like a warm breeze on a mid-winter day, they melted the frost surrounding his heart. There had always been something about those eyes...something that made everything okay... at least for just a bit. "Maybe everybody's been right," Lester mused. "Maybe I've been too tough on the kid."

"How's it going, Dad?" Lex repeated.

Roused from his hypnotic stupor, Lester replied, "It's great to see you, son! How are you?"

"I'm cool," Lex smiled.

"How's it going over at your mom's?" Dad inquired.

"Awe, good," Lex answered, "I needed some wheels so that I could find a job. Mom signed the loan so that I could get this ride. It's only got 15,000 miles on it, and it's got the high output V8!"

Those baby blues were still at work.

Lex continued, "Now she's getting all uptight because it's taking me a little longer than I thought to find a job. Now winter's on the way, and she's all bent out of shape about helping me buy snow tires...and I'm a little behind on the payments."

In a semi-hypnotic state, Dad inquired, "How much do you need?"

Lex mumbled, "About a grand or two is all."

"Oh gosh," Lester stuttered, "I...I... don't know. That's a... a...a lot of cash."

Lex flashed those peepers and turned on the guilt, "You know how dangerous these roads can be in the winter. And how am I going to find a job if I can't even get to interviews?"

Lonnie called out the front door, "Lester? Who's there? Is that Lex?"

Lex leaped behind the wheel. "Dad I've got to go. Hey, I'll give you a call tomorrow."

Dad dodged the bullet...at least for the moment.

Love is an awesome thing! More powerful than an a-bomb, it can move mountains and bring even the mightiest parent to their knees. If you love your kids...and I'm quite certain you do...you've felt that horrible tug on your heart strings. It's easy to think about saying "No"—that is, until you look into their eyes. It's easy to talk a big game about getting tough and expecting your kids to become responsible...that is, until the rubber hits the pavement.

Parenting would be far easier if our kids were strangers. Love wouldn't confuse our logic, and there wouldn't be any dysfunctional patterns to slip into. Lex and his father had rehearsed their waltz so many times that they immediately hit the dance floor anytime they occupied the same space. Dad would start with a feeble attempt to act tough. Lex would counter with a flash of those eyes and just a dash of guilt. The whole thing would wrap up with Dad giving in...and Lonnie blasting off like a bottle rocket on the Fourth of July.

Parenting would be far easier if our kids were strangers. Love wouldn't confuse our logic, and there wouldn't be any dysfunctional patterns to slip into.

The fifth "E" of Love and Logic stands for Empathy. Lonnie relayed none of it as Lester told her that he was considering giving Lex the cash.

"You have got to be kidding!" Lonnie lost it. "You're thinking about doing what?"

"Well, the snow's going to fly before long," Lester defended. "He's got to have some sort of safe transportation if he's going to find a job."

Lonnie wasn't subtle. "That's the stupidest thing I've ever heard!"

Believe it or not, this didn't bring the best out of Lester. "It's easy to sit there and be critical! You never stop to see my side of this situation. Do you think this is just that simple? Well, it's not!"

Twenty-four hours later, Lex had a check signed by his loving father.

Thirty-six hours later, Lonnie was trying to decide whether she would visit Dr. Couch...or a divorce attorney. Fortunately, she opted for the good doctor.

"So...let me make sure that I've got this right," queried Dr. Couch. "Lex comes over and sweet talks his dad. Then you blow up. Then Dad gets defensive, pouts, and self-medicates by being the hero."

"Self-medicates?" Lonnie asked. "What's that mean?"

"Well," the doctor continued, "it sounds like Lester finds it pretty soothing to bail out his son. Even though he knows down deep that it's the wrong thing to do, it makes him better in the short term."

"Kinda like an alcoholic taking a drink?" Lonnie asked.

"Yeah, sort of like that," Dr. Couch replied. "And there's another problem here. When Lester feels hammered by you, it makes him more likely to need a fix. When people experience anger, guilt, fear, or any uncomfortable emotion, they have a hard time making good decisions. The more intense the emotion, the more difficult it becomes for them to solve problems. Instead of doing things that result in long-term positive results, they do whatever it takes to feel better in the short term."

"So," Liz asked, "yelling at Lester is making it even harder for him to do the right thing?"

Dr Couch grinned, "You're one of my brightest pupils!"

From Dr. Couch, Lonnie learned that empathy is the key to helping Lester make better decisions about his son. If she can use this powerful skill, he'll find it easier to use it with his son. There's an added benefit! If Lex sees his dad staying calm and using empathy with him, he'll be more likely to stay calm and make good decisions himself. Yes! Each time we use empathy with others, we teach it to them through modeling. We also give them a glimpse of the attitudes possessed by the world's greatest thinkers and leaders:

- Great problem-solvers think, "Oh man…that didn't work so well. I wonder what I could try instead?"
- Poor ones throw a stink. "Why does something always go wrong? Nothing ever works out. Why won't anybody help me out?"
- Great problem-solvers ponder, "What a challenge! It'll be interesting to see how we solve this."

- Poor ones pout, "This is so frustrating. This should have never happened! It's not fair!"
- Great problem-solvers wonder, "What am I supposed to learn from this? What could I do the next time?"
- Poor problem-solvers whine, "I can't do anything right! Nobody cares. If they did, they'd help me out."

**Each time we use empathy with others,
we teach it to them through modeling.**

The way we interpret problems...the thoughts that go through our head...has a profound impact on our ability to entertain and apply creative solutions. Oversimplified, the human brain is composed of two basic areas: the frontal cortex and the brain stem. The frontal cortex does the thinking. The brain stem does the reacting. The frontal cortex analyzes new information, accesses old learning, and combines it all in a way that enables us to come up with creative courses of action. It also allows us to evaluate the likely consequences of these actions and to use this information to make good decisions. The brain stem is all about basic survival...that is, fight or flight. When we interpret problems in ways that create anxiety, fear, or anger, the frontal cortex shuts down, our thinking narrowly focuses on just one or two actions, and we become lizard-like in our thinking.

Yes! Many psychologists refer to the brain stem as the "reptilian brain." Reptile behavior is primarily reactionary and rooted in basic survival drives. That's why geckos, monitor lizards, alligators, and komodo dragons make very poor employees. Sadly, many people are raised in such a way that they completely lose their creative thinking abilities anytime something goes wrong. They panic, they give up, they compulsively repeat the same ineffective behaviors, or they adopt a victim mentality. They act like Lester and Lex.

Geckos, monitor lizards, alligators, and komodo dragons make very poor employees. They're also ill equipped to participate as responsible citizens of our country.

Lonnie learned that each time she yelled at her husband for being wimpy, she made it more likely that he'd fall back on old, ineffective patterns. The more anxious, defensive, or angry Lester felt about the situation, the more likely he'd rely on what felt good in the short term…instead of what was best for the long term. The more Lex was rescued from his irresponsible behavior, the more he needed to be rescued. To break this dysfunctional family cycle, Lonnie had to find a way to stay calm herself.

"But…how do I do it?" Lonnie asked Dr. Couch. "I mean… I'm so frustrated about all of this that I can't think straight."

"Is this a horrible, terrible situation?" asked the doctor.

"It feels that way to me!" Lonnie lamented.

"Is this the end of the world?" Dr. Couch inquired.

"I'm fit to be tied!" Lonnie replied.

Rising from her chair, Dr. Couch sighed, "Well, I guess it's best to give up."

"What are you talking about?" Lonnie complained.

"I'm trying to make a point," smiled the doctor. "How will you solve this problem if you continue to think of it as something horrible…instead of a challenge in need of a solution?"

Finding it difficult to conceal her annoyance, Lonnie asked, "What am I supposed to do?"

Dr. Couch continued, "When we're trying to bust out of old habits, the first step involves clearly visualizing the way we want to behave instead. If we can't see it, we can't be it."

"What do you mean?" Lonnie asked.

"What do you want to look and sound like when Lester starts slipping into his old patterns with Lex?" the doctor inquired.

"I really wish I didn't get so upset. I know that's not helping. I guess I...I guess that I really don't know what to do, instead."

Dr. Couch handed her a well-worn CD case. "This is going to give you a way of changing your reactions when things start to go wrong with Lester and Lex. Listen to this at least six times over the next week. Next week we'll practice and get you ready to give it a shot."

During that next week, Lonnie listened to the Love and Logic CD, The Four Steps to Responsibility, six times. By Friday, she was sick and tired of hearing the same old thing...

Lock in a strong dose of empathy first...like, 'this is such a bummer' or 'how sad.' Then hand the problem back by asking, 'What do you think you are going to do?' Then ask, 'Would you like to hear some ideas?' Remember to say, 'Some kids decide to_____. How would that work for you?' as you give one or two ideas for solving the problem. Then just end by saying, 'Good luck. Let me know how that works out."

By her next session with Dr. Couch, Lonnie was confused. "Why did you give me a CD about kids?" Lonnie asked. "I know that Lester sometimes acts like a kid, but will this really work with an adult?"

"You bet!" the doctor replied. "In fact, it even works with the other psychologists I supervise. If it'll work on a shrink, it'll work on anyone!"

After practicing it with Dr. Couch, Lonnie couldn't wait for an opportunity to use it with her husband! It wasn't long before that opportunity presented itself. Something about the way the phone rang told her that Lex was going to be on the other end of the line. Sure enough, when she answered, all she heard was silence, followed by, "Uh...is my dad there?"

Though she heard only one side of the conversation, she knew exactly what was going down. "Gosh, Lex...that's a lot of money," she heard her husband mumble. "What did your mom say?"

In the past, she would've cast Lester a look capable of incinerating hardened steel. This time was different. She actually felt sad for the old guy, particularly when she heard him stumble, ""Well...um...uh...I'm going to have to...Lex...I know that you need it now...but...Lex...I...uh...well..."

Later that evening, she couldn't resist asking, "Honey, what's Lex up to these days? How's he doing?"

The bulging veins on Lester's forehead told much of the story, "He's late on his car payments, and he had a big fight with his mom about it. She kicked him out of the house, and now he's living with his grandfather."

Instead of launching into her traditional "don't-think-about-sending-him-money-for-crying-out-loud" lecture, she replied, "That's too bad. I bet that's tough to hear."

Lester's expression was priceless...like he'd just seen Elvis at the supermarket, "Uh...yeah...it's really disappointing."

"I bet," Lonnie agreed.

"And his mom stopped making his car payments," Lester continued. "If he doesn't come up with seven grand by Wednesday, they're going to repossess it."

Remembering what she'd learned from the CD, Lonnie asked, "So, what do you think you are going to do?"

Much to her amusement, Lester responded just like a child. Shrugging his shoulders, he replied, "I don't know."

"Would you like some ideas?" Lonnie inquired.

"I just don't know what I'm going to do with him;" Lester lamented, "it's like he never learns his lesson. I've tried everything with him, and nothing works."

Lonnie continued, "Well, I guess that some parents would just give him the money. How do you think that might work?"

"He just wastes every dime I give him," Lester replied. "He's got no respect for money!"

"Some parents would let their kid learn a life lesson by allowing the car to get repossessed," Lonnie continued. "How would that work out?"

"Oh…he'd be furious at me!" Lester answered.

"I know," Lonnie empathized. "That's always a bad feeling. Honey, I'll love you regardless of what you decide to do about this. Would you like one more idea?"

Lester was curious, "What?"

"Some parents remember that it's okay for their kids to be upset in the short term so that they can be more responsible in the long term. I've been listening to this CD. It talks about how to do this. Feel free to listen to it if you'd like."

"I don't know," Lester sighed, "I just wish he'd grow up!"

"I know," she agreed. "I'll love you no matter what you decide. Good luck."

She did it! The ball was now in his court!

Two days later the phone rang. From the other room, she overheard the conversation. "Lex, I know that losing your car must be really upsetting. What are you going to do?"

She couldn't believe her ears! He was actually using the stuff!

"Some people decide to see if their friends will loan them any money," he continued, "Do you think that might work?"

She still couldn't believe it!

"Other people decide to ride the bus to work," he suggested.

Now she could actually hear Lex's screams coming through the receiver.

Shaken yet determined, Lester wrapped up the call, "Lex, I will love you no matter what you decide. Let me know how this works out. Good luck."

Although there are no guarantees that our kids will make the right decisions when we apply these skills, the odds go way up. Lex spent many months feeling disgruntled with his father, and his father spent many months wondering if he'd really done the right thing. Lex lost his convertible, but he gained something much greater: an opportunity to see that he could make it in life without being rescued. Many years later…and after having many more real work learning experiences…he admitted to his father that riding the bus back and forth from an honest day's work produced far greater self-respect than driving that shiny car he'd acquired through whining and manipulation.

CHAPTER SIX

My Manager Follows Me Everywhere!

Teach your kids to lead rather than follow.

Terri grew up in a typical neighborhood around lots of typical kids from typical families with typical problems. Almost every day she met the typical temptations youngsters face as she walked to and from school, played at the park, hung out with her friends, etc.

"Come on, Terri. Just grab the answer sheet off of Mrs. Green's desk. We'll put it back before she even knows it's missing."

"Come on, Terri. We dare you to kiss Tommy Turner."

"Come on, Terri. Let's skip class. What are you afraid of?"

When Terri left home for college, those temptations didn't go away…and they sure didn't get any smaller! They just kept coming…

"Come on, Terri. It's just a little weed. Everybody's doing it. What's the matter? Are you scared?"

"Come on, Terri. I love you. If you really loved me you wouldn't be so hung up about making love."

"Come on, Terri. All you have to do is text message the exam answers to my cell. It's no big deal."

When Terri finished her master's degree and was hired by J.R. Colby and Associates Investment Brokers, did the temptations cease? Not a chance! Hiding behind every corner was another. Occasionally, insider trading information came leaking down the grapevine. There were always opportunities to make exaggerated claims about investment opportunities just to grab a commission. There were plenty of chances to bilk folks out of more cash by charging them for plenty of unnecessary trades. There were even opportunities to get rich quick by selling securities that didn't even exist!

Like all business owners and managers, there was no way that J.R. Colby could keep an eye on all of his employees all of the time. There was no way that he could follow their every move, making certain that they always did what was right. That's why he took so much care hiring...and promoting...people like Terri. Early in her life, long before she'd ever heard of a mutual fund or a diversified portfolio, she'd developed a little voice in her head that constantly nagged, "Terri? Are you listening? Terri! Have you thought about how the decision you are about to make will turn out? Have you considered the consequences? How will you feel about yourself? Remember how sad it was when you stole that quarter from Mom's purse when you were five? Remember what happened? Terri, the quality of your life depends on it!"

Early in her life, Terri's parents realized that they weren't going to be able to follow her everywhere, forever making sure that she did the right thing. Since hiring a body guard or a personal manager to do this didn't seem practical, they came to grips with the fact that Terri needed to learn this job herself. Yep, if their sweet little daughter was going to survive and thrive in this temptation-laden world, she would need to develop a mobile manager...one residing between her ears and in her heart...that would guide her every step.

Sobering as it may be, we're all like Terri's parents. We're all in the same boat. Regardless of how energetic, resourceful, or caring we are, we'll never be capable of following our kids through their daily lives, ensuring that they always make good decisions. Parents who try find themselves completely exhausted. They also create kids who fall prey to peer pressure. Why? Simply because they've been conditioned to believe that they can't think for themselves.

Self-control is the greatest gift we can give our kids! Self-control is what this entire book is about. If we can raise kids with mobile managers inside of their heads, they're guaranteed to achieve great success in the workplace and in life. Employers understand that the very best employees are those who have the self-control to effectively manage themselves. America's survival rests on our ability to raise more citizens with this ability! In this final chapter, we'll pull everything together and see how the five E's of Love and Logic provide the foundation for raising kids who do the right thing even when it's not the easy thing.

Employers understand that the very best employees are those who have the self-control to effectively manage themselves. America's survival rests on our ability to raise more citizens with this ability!

Example

"What do we get if we're good in the store?" whined little Sammy Scott.

"Yeah, it's been so long since we got anything new!" sister Stevie sassed.

Hearing this for the 113th time that week, their loving mother lost it. Slamming the shopping cart into park, her eyes glowed red and smoke billowed out of her nostrils. "I am sick and tired of hearing that! Quit asking! You guys have so many toys at home that you can't even play with them all. You know—"

Just as she was getting to the best part of her lecture...the part about kids who don't even have any toys to play with...little Sammy interrupted, "Yeah, but, what do we get?"

Stevie jumped in as well, "Yeah...can we get that movie about that witch that's really a princess?"

"Didn't you hear a word I said?" Mom exploded. "I TOLD YOU NO!"

A little tear trickled down sweet Sammy's cheek. A second one dribbled off his sister's. Choking on more of them, they cried in unison, "Yeah...but...but...we thought you loved us. Besides, you always get what you want."

That afternoon, the little Scott sweeties skipped out of the store with lollypops in their mouths and a DVD movie about a witch that was really a princess.

Mrs. Scott rationalized, "Well...I guess it really isn't fair if they see me buying nice things for myself...and they don't get something, too."

A year later, things weren't any better.

Sammy spouted, "Tyler's dad's car has two DVD players in the back."

Stevie concurred, "Yeah, Dad. It's really cool. Why does ours just have one?"

Dad grumbled, "Some cars don't have two...uh...I don't know. It's not like you guys can't just share."

Two weeks later, Mr. Scott's car had two backseat DVD players, too!

A couple years later, all seemed right with the world...at least according to the kids.

"Dad?" Sammy inquired, "how come we don't have cell phones like other kids? I'm seven!"

Stevie jumped in, "Yeah, all the other kids in third grade have one. Abby has one! What would happen if there was an emergency? How would we call you? Besides, you always get what you want. You get to have a new one every year, but we don't even get any." "Uh," Dad grunted, "I guess that it would be good if you could get a hold of us."

A year later, the snowball continued to roll downhill.

"Mom! Mom! Dad! Dad!" Sammy screamed. "Why aren't you guys listening to us?"

Stevie joined in, "Yeah! These phones are boring! They don't even take pictures. And…why can't we text? Why didn't you get the plan with texting? You guys have ones that text, and Mom's plays MP3 downloads."

It wasn't long before Sammy and his sis were texting, taking snapshots, and tuning in to their favorite digital downloads.

Six months later, they'd trashed those phones and needed new ones.

One year later, Mrs. Scott overheard something exceptionally upsetting.

"Did you see that new girl named Becky?" Stevie whispered with eyes rolling back in her skull.

Sammy scoffed, "Yeah…like her clothes look like she got 'em at a garage sale."

"And her hair is so weird," Stevie giggled cruelly. "She never washes it. I wonder if she even owns a brush."

Mom's heart ached as she continued to listen.

"Yeah, and did you see the car her mom dropped her off in?" Sammy snorted. "It's got rust holes all over it, and it looks like it's from the nineties or something."

"Yeah," Stevie sneered, "it's like her clothes."

That night Mrs. Scott got very little sleep. In the morning she finally woke up and smelled the coffee…the pot that'd been burning on the warmer for the last twelve years. The clouds of denial parted. It was clear as day. She had two extremely cold, self-centered youngsters living under her roof.

What does the self-centeredness of the Scott siblings have to do with the topic of this chapter? What can their arrogance and selfishness teach us about our goal of raising kids with mobile managers?

Here's the bottom line: When kids grow to believe that they deserve only the best, they come to believe that they are truly superior to others. They also begin to believe that they are above having to follow the rules. The older they get, the more they think:

I deserve the best because I'm so special. In fact, I'm far more special than anybody else! Because I'm so special, I'm entitled to all I want. In fact, I'm so worthy of special treatment that it's okay if I bend...or break...the rules. Besides, those rules were made for regular people...not super special people like me.

When temptations float their way, folks with this attitude reason:

Sure, I know that this is against the rules, but those rules weren't made for me. I'm special! Sure, I know that this might harm someone else, but they deserve it because they aren't special like me. If they were special like me, bad things wouldn't happen to them.

The number of people possessing this poisonous character flaw has reached epic proportions! People with this mindset think nothing of buying gold trash cans and spending millions of dollars on birthday parties with the money they've stolen from honest, hardworking people. In today's self-centered, ultra-materialistic world, how do we raise kids who understand that the quality of one's ethics is far more important than the quality of one's car? How do we create children who believe that the size of a person's conscience is far more important than the size of their house? The first "E" of Love and Logic stands for Example. The Smiths were about to learn how this powerful tool could turn the tide in their home. Before we see how, let's review what we've learned about the first "E" so far.

In chapter 1, June learned to be a great model by…

- Realizing that she couldn't set a good example unless she was taking good care of herself in loving, unselfish ways.
- Setting appropriate limits without anger, lectures, threats, or repeated warnings.
- Spending most of her time and energy focusing on her own behavior…rather than her daughter Patty's.

In chapter 2, Mr. Hammer…

- Learned that when he complained about work in front of Max he was inadvertently teaching his son that getting a good education leads to unhappiness.
- Realized that what our kids overhear is far more powerful than what we tell them directly.
- Learned to talk with great excitement about his job when Max was nearby.

In chapter 3, Ruby realized that…

- Her kids were learning to be negative about life by watching her and listening to her complaining.
- One way to feel better and set a more positive example is to experiment with acting like a positive person.
- Her kids were far easier to get along with when she was focusing on the positive.

In chapter 4, Mr. and Mrs. Peterson…

- Learned that trying to be perfect in front of their son, Peter, was sending him the message that mistakes are horrible.

- Realized that his perfectionism was standing in the way of his achievement.
- Found out that they could turn this problem around by modeling plenty of mistakes in front of him.

In chapter 5, we saw…

- How children learn to solve problems by watching their parents solve problems.
- Why it's so important to involve our kids in daily household tasks and maintenance.
- How to model problem-solving skills by thinking out loud when our kids are nearby.

Mrs. Scott cried on her husband's shoulder, "I've turned them into egotistical little brats! I know it's my fault!"

"What are you talking about?" he begged.

"It's my fault that they look down their noses at others," she sobbed, "I know it is. When I was growing up, I always felt like everybody else was prettier and had nicer things. I never wanted them to feel the way I did."

"There's nothing wrong with wanting a nice life for them," he tried to reassure. "Besides, I don't think it's your fault."

"I know it is," she countered. "I know that I do it. I think it's because down deep I still feel like a dirty little poor kid living in a run-down trailer park."

"What?" he questioned.

"I know I do it in front of them," she continued. "I talk down about people. Like when I'm driving and I see a worn out car. Or sometimes I say nasty things about how people dress, or their house, or their poor taste. It's like when I do it, it makes me feel better about myself for just a little while."

Mr. Scott kept his lips clamped firmly together...so that the thoughts inside of his head wouldn't leak out. "She's got a point," he thought. "She does say things like that in front of the kids...a lot of the time. Should I agree with her? No...that's a bad idea. Maybe I could change the subject or something...yeah..."

Before he could speak, his lovely wife foiled the plan, "And don't try to change the subject. I can tell what you are thinking. You always try to change the subject when we're talking about things like this!"

Between a hard place and solid granite, he blurted, "Yeah... okay...you do say things like that around the kids...but...it's not like it's that big of a—"

"Yes it is a big deal," she interrupted. "I've heard you do it, too. I've been reading this book that talks all about how kids gain most of their attitudes from overhearing what we say. It's like the guy wrote it with us in mind. It's like we're in the book. He also talks about how kids who think they are better than others end up having a tough time following the rules."

"So what are we supposed to do?" Mr. Scott whined.

"We need to get in the habit of saying more positive things about others in front of the kids," she answered. "In the book, it suggests writing some examples on little sticky notes and putting them where you will see them a lot...like on the bathroom mirror, on your alarm clock, on the steering wheel of the car... places like that."

Now he was getting irritated. "I really don't think this is such a big deal. It seems like every time you read a new book, you start second-guessing yourself. The kids are fine. There's nothing wrong with them feeling good about themselves. What's wrong with that?"

Mrs. Scott swallowed the words she really wanted to say and continued. "Another thing I learned in this book is that parents don't always need to have the same parenting style. I'm going to make some changes. I will love you even if you don't."

Mr. Scott suddenly remembered that he had lots of projects waiting for him in the garage. "Oh, the garage…" mused his subconscious, "that sanctuary of manhood, where men are never weighted with the worries of the world…like hygiene, deep thoughts, or personal growth."

That weekend, Mrs. Scott loaded the kids in the car and headed downtown.

"Where are we going?" demanded Stevie.

"I'll let you know when we get there," Mom replied. "We're going to do something very, very important."

"Yeah, but why are we going this way?" Sammy questioned. "There's nothing down here except for a bunch of bums and nasty old buildings."

As they parked outside of the 7th Street Shelter, the kids were freaked. "Mom! What are we doing here? What's going on?"

Mom finally spilled the beans. "I've been horribly selfish," she confided.

Stevie was perplexed, "Huh?"

Sammy was puzzled, "What?"

Their lovely mother continued, "I've had such a good life, that I've forgotten that there are a lot of families that aren't as fortunate as ours. Sure, your dad and I have worked very hard, but I've forgotten that it's only by the grace of God that we have what we have. We are going to start spending more time giving back by helping others."

Too shocked to speak, the Scott siblings shuffled into the building behind their mother. As the day unfolded, they helped peel potatoes, chop carrots, shuck corn, and prepare meals for those who don't have cell phones with MP3 players or duel backseat DVDs. As they worked, they watched their mother. As they watched they learned a little lesson about humility, gratitude, and the pride that comes from giving.

Allowing our kids to overhear us speaking positively about others is critical. Through this healthy example, they learn to respect others, respect rules, and to value the blessings they've been given. By regularly involving them in volunteer activities... and letting them see our joy as we work alongside...we super-charge this first "E" of Love and Logic!

There are few things more therapeutic than helping others in need. In fact, Mrs. Smith felt so great that she wasn't even discouraged when she heard her youngsters complaining on the way home.

There are few things more therapeutic than helping others in need.

"I'm glad that's over!" Sammy pronounced.

Stevie agreed, "Yeah. That was so boring!"

"That was like three hours," Sammy added. "What do we get for doing all that stuff?"

Jumping on the bandwagon, Stevie demanded, "Yeah, what do we get?"

Have you ever noticed how kids seem to learn the most important lessons in life slower than we want them to? As the car rolled along, Mom reminded herself that this lesson was worth the wait...and worth the hard work. With great love in her voice, she asked, "You guys are wondering what you're going to get?"

"Yeah!" both shouted.

"You've already got it," Mom answered.

"What is it? What did we get?" they asked with wild anticipation.

Keeping both eyes on the road, Mom replied, "The pride of knowing that you did something for someone in need."

Stevie slumped down in the seat. Sammy did the same. Neither of them congratulated their mother on her newly acquired parental prowess!

Expectation

Ms. Skinner was ready to start her teaching career by having the very best behaved class at J.B. Watson elementary school. In college she'd learned that behavior that's rewarded increases while behavior that isn't decreases. "With just the right types of rewards," she told herself, "I won't have all of those behavior problems seen by other teachers. All I have to do is create the right system with the right types of rewards."

She'd spent her entire summer thumbing through her behavior modification text books. With great care she reasoned, "The first step in creating my system is to decide what I want my students to do. My professors called these 'target behaviors.' Let's see…"

On a crisp, clean piece of paper she wrote:

- Walk in the hall
- Keep your hands and feet to yourself
- Raise your hand and wait to be called on before speaking
- Come to class prepared with all necessary materials
- Treat each other with respect
- Respect the property of others
- Complete assignments by the date due
- Stand quietly when in line
- Etc.

Now Ms. Skinner was ready for the fun part. "What types of rewards should I give the kids for doing these things?" she pondered. "Let's see…"

- Regular stickers
- Scratch and sniff stickers
- Special pencils and pencil toppers
- Extra computer time

- Candy
- Praise
- Those neat little erasers shaped like different objects
- Extra free time
- Pizza parties
- Etc.

"Now," she thought, "all I have to do is make some sort of chart for my bulletin board so that the students know how all of this will work."

It was a beauty!

By the first day of school Ms. Skinner was ready to rock and roll…and reward! With great joy she rushed over to little Rhoda Reuben and handed her a sticker that read, "STAR!"

"You raised your hand and waited to be called on!" Ms. Skinner cheered.

Rhoda beamed with pride.

Later that day, Ms. Skinner spied Alex Alexander standing quietly in line. "You are standing so quietly and patiently!" she congratulated. "You just earned a candy."

Popping the piece into his mouth, he mumbled, "Thanks."

The next day, Joey Jamerson got a 100 on his spelling test. That earned him thirty minutes of extra computer time.

Mandy Moon earned three glitter covered pencils for keeping her hands to herself.

Polite Patty Paulson said "please" and "thank you," netting her a nifty eraser shaped like the Statue of Liberty.

During that glorious first week of school, Ms. Skinner dispensed 23 stickers, 36 pieces of candy, 17 glitter-covered pencils, two hours of extra computer time, and countless nifty little erasers shaped like the Statue of Liberty. It was a banner week indeed!

This wasn't a surprise to Ms. Skinner. "It just makes sense," she thought, recalling what she'd learned in the ivory tower.

"Behavior that's rewarded increases while behavior that isn't decreases. It's just that simple."

Or is it?

The first hint of trouble came the third week of school when Joey Jamerson earned a glittery pencil for remembering that "i" comes before "e" except after "c."

"That's great! Ms. Skinner congratulated.

Joey was less than excited. "Ms. Skinner. These pencils are really cheap. The erasers fall off even when you don't rub hard. Can't I just go on the computer, instead?"

More cracks in the plan surfaced when Rhoda Reuben earned another "STAR!" sticker.

"Awe, man!" she complained. "I already have one of these. Patty got one of those Statue of Liberty erasers. Why do I just get a crumby sticker?"

Ms. Skinner was at a loss for words. "How can this be?" she pondered. "Behavior that's rewarded increases while behavior that isn't decreases."

Ms. Skinner's behavior modification world crumbled around her as she attempted to coax Mandy Moon into finishing her math. "What will you give me if I do it?" Mandy negotiated.

Ms. Skinner was out of Statue erasers. Her remaining glittery pencils had undergone inadvertent eraser-lectomies. There was no space at the computer stations. Her stickers had lost their appeal. The only remaining reward was one semi-melted candy with a piece of hair stuck to it.

"I don't want that!" Mandy moaned. "It's old!"

The Second "E" of Love and Logic stands for Expectation. In her well-intentioned yet misguided attempts to apply the time-honored principles of behavior modification, Ms. Skinner had communicated the expectation that her students could not be-have and do the right thing without getting the right things. As we already know, it rarely takes long for children to either live up to…or down to…our expectations. Now they were firmly convinced that they were entitled to goodies each and every time they did something good. When children develop this, "What's in this for me?" world view, their behavior is less guided by internal standards of morality than the rewards dangled in front of their noses. Self-control becomes secondary.

> **When children develop a, "What's in this for me?" world view, their behavior is less guided by internal standards of morality than the rewards dangled in front of their noses.**

The trend began in the 1950's, when some parents and educators got hooked on the idea that research on rats, mice, monkeys, and pigeons could be applied to children. From this research, many hoped that the liberal use of rewards would end their child-rearing and pedagogical woes. Since rewards often result in quick behavioral improvement, many adults became addicts…and the trend turned into a full-fledged societal makeover. Practically everyone seemed to jump on the goodie-giving and praise-pushing bandwagon. No classroom seemed complete without a reward chart. Educators and parents became cheerleaders. "Super!" "That's great!" "You are wonderful!" became their mantra.

Now we've got a mess on our hands.

Employers are feeling the pain. America's feeling the pain. We're all feeling the pain! Our great country is sinking under the weight of a population who largely believes that only fools do things for free. The walls are crumbling because of the sheer number of people who believe that they are entitled to massive rewards for miniscule work. While disturbing, this sad state of affairs presents an amazing opportunity for those who're committed to raising people who believe that success comes from hard work and dedication…rather than handouts. Before we dive into how modifying our expectations can help us toward this goal, I'd better deal with some probable dissention.

Our great country is sinking under the weight of a population who largely believes that only fools do things for free.

Yes! I bet some of you are hopping mad. I'm sure a few of you are furious! If you're trained in behavior modification...as I am...you may be thinking, "Where does he get off spouting this sort of sewage? The research is clear! Behavior modification rests on a secure foundation of empirically-validated principles. For years I've had great results using rewards. They better give me a refund on this book!"

Among educators and parenting experts, few topics arouse more passion than the debate between the "anti-reward activist" and "sticker commando" camps. The anti-reward folks believe that the use of rewards always creates selfish kids who're addicted to goodies. Sticker commandos believe that children should always receive praise and tangible rewards each and every time they behave. Both camps cite convincing research to support their position.

As I've aged...and hopefully matured...I've seen that each of these perspectives is short-sighted. Those with wisdom understand that each child and situation is unique. Sometimes rewards can be an effective tool. Sometimes they aren't. Because they understand the following risks of rewards, they apply them with great care, only when the situation seems right:

- *Focusing on rewards can distract us from building sincere, positive relationships.*
  I've witnessed many well-meaning parents and educators who've become so focused on finding the right reward that

they'd forgotten the importance of building positive relationships with kids. When children believe we don't care, rewards feel like bribes.

- *Rewards fail to address the underlying causes of behavior.*
  While rewards may modify the observable behavior, the underlying problem often remains.

- *With strong-willed or oppositional kids, rewards often create power struggles.*
  Rewards send the message, "I want you to do this so badly that I will give you something if you will do it."

  It's quite typical for extremely stubborn kids to think, "Now that I know what he wants, I'll do the opposite. Who cares about that crumby reward? It's gonna be a whole lot more exciting to see his face turn red!"

- *Focusing on rewards can be exhausting and stressful.*
  I've been truly saddened by the number of educators and parents I've seen who could no longer enjoy their kids because they're working so hard to keep track of points, checkmarks, tokens, stickers, or some other type of reward.

- *Used unwisely, rewards foster selfishness and a dependence on external controls rather than self-control.*
  Ms. Skinner was beginning to learn this lesson!

Fortunately, there's great hope for those who've unintentionally hooked their kids on this ego-centric perspective. By applying the second "E" of Love and Logic, Expectation, we can turn this around.

Before we see how Ms. Skinner stops the bleeding, let's review what we've learned about this second "E" so far...

In Chapter 1, June learned that...

- High expectations are communicated through solid limits.
- The key to setting enforceable limits involves describing what we are going to do or allow...rather trying to tell our kids what to do.
- Her daughter became capable of meeting high expectations when she became ready and willing to provide them.

In Chapter 2, Mr. Hammer...

- Learned that low expectations in the form of overprotection were eroding his son Max's sense of personal responsibility and self-worth.
- Saw that countless parents across our great nation are taking this to such an extreme that they are showing up in bosses' offices, attempting to negotiate better jobs for their adult children.
- Learned there is great hope if we are willing to send high expectations by resisting the urge to solve all of our children's problems for them.

In Chapter 3, Ruby realized...

- That always trying to be a "nice mommy," who never set limits, was communicating low expectations and allowing her kids to walk all over her.
- That sometimes parents need to go on strike and negotiate for better working conditions.
- How helpful it can be to say, "I'll be happy to do the extra things I do for you when I feel respected...and your chores are done."

In Chapter 4, Liz and Lester found out…

- That expecting to achieve "perfect parent" status was setting them up for feeling frustrated and depressed when their kids acted up or made mistakes.
- How all of this frustration actually communicates to our children that we aren't capable of handling them.
- That we're far more effective when we expect that our kids will make mistakes while simultaneously expecting that they have what it takes to learn from them.

In Chapter 5, we saw that…

- Successful parents remember that their most important job is to raise children who don't need them.
- Healthy parents, like Gloria, find it simpler to expect independent, responsible behavior because they don't depend on their kids to meet their own emotional needs.
- Down deep kids really appreciate being expected to own and solve their problems.

Let's get back to Ms. Skinner and her class. That Monday morning, they all sat at their desks in utter disbelief. Patty Paulson was perplexed, and little Mandy Moon moaned. Alex Alexander asked, "Ms. Skinner? What happened to this place this weekend?"

The walls seemed empty without her reward chart. Rhoda Rueben raised her hand…and opened her mouth at precisely the same moment, "Teacher! Teacher! Somebody stole your poster!"

Smiling warmly, Ms. Skinner replied, "Oh…thanks for noticing. I did it. I took it down."

"But why?" queried the class.

Ms. Skinner continued, "I'm very sorry for expecting so little out of you guys."

Now they were really confused!

"I'm sorry for thinking that you would only behave if I gave you stickers, pencils, or other types of rewards. Over the weekend I realized that I haven't been giving you enough credit for how good you really are."

Their little mouths hung open in disbelief.

"I'm going to do things a lot differently now," she promised. "I'm going to stop treating you like little kids by giving you all of this stuff every time you do something good."

Joey Jamerson jumped to his feet, "Yeah but...but...what do we get if we're really, really, really good?"

"A good feeling inside yourself!" Ms. Skinner answered with great perkiness. "There's nothing that makes me feel better than doing a great job. I just love that feeling!"

Mandy Moon interrupted, "No way Ms. S! We ain't gonna get nothin'?"

Still smiling, Ms. Skinner replied, "I've learned that people tend to enjoy nice things a lot more when they come as a surprise. So...sometimes when I see that one of you is doing something really good...and isn't expecting anything for doing it...it'll make me feel so proud that I'll want to reward them with something."

Over the previous weekend, Ms. Skinner realized that she was communicating very low expectations for her students by believing that they needed to be rewarded for every good deed. In essence, she was saying to them, "Students, you are all so morally corrupt...and have such little self-respect...that I've got to bribe you into behaving."

**We communicate very low expectations
for our kids when we believe that they must
be rewarded for every good deed.**

As we learned early in this book, children will always live up to...or down to...our expectations.

Ms. Skinner realized something else. She'd ignored one of the most powerful and practical principles of behavior modification:

**Unexpected rewards tend to have far more power
than expected ones.**

That's right! When we come to expect a reward…and we know exactly when we will get it…the reward soon loses its effectiveness. Psychologist types call this a "fixed schedule of reinforcement." It's "fixed" because the person receiving it always knows when it will arrive. Ms. Skinner quickly learned that her fixed schedule of reinforcement simply created kids who'd only work long enough or hard enough to get what they wanted.

"Variable schedule of reinforcement" is the term commonly used to describe rewards that come as a surprise. Reviewing her behavior modification text books, Ms. Skinner was reminded that these sorts of schedules keep children guessing as to when they may be rewarded. Most of the time, no rewards are given for good behavior. This gives them an opportunity to experience the internal pride associated with achievement. It also prevents them from developing the belief that they are entitled to constant praise and goodies.

Ms. Skinner was excited about her new and more practical approach. Her students still weren't sure what to think! Reminding herself that change is hard, she prepared herself for things to get a bit rougher in the short term. "It's like remodeling your home," a friend reassured her. "For things to get nicer in the long term they have to get uglier in the short term."

Education

Mr. Scott's heart sank as he listened to his son complain about his teacher.

"She's so lame," Sammy spouted. "Today she went on this long lecture about how we shouldn't always expect to get stuff every time we do something good."

"Well...Sammy," Dad replied, "she's got a point. I think it would be pretty sad if people only did good things when they knew they'd be paid for them."

"Dad," sighed Sammy, "you just don't understand. Besides, you get paid at your job."

Lost for words, Mr. Scott tried to change the subject. "How's your friend Joey Jamerson?"

"He's cool," Sammy replied, "but Ms. Skinner is always on our case. It's like she gets all bent out of shape anytime we want to talk to each other. Yesterday she made me sit up front...just because she says that we talk too much. That's so unfair."

Feeling a need to say something parental, Dad furled his brow and grumbled, "You really need to listen to your teachers. Besides, if Joey is getting you in that much trouble, you'd better think twice about having him as a friend!"

Slamming his bedroom door behind him, Sammy spewed, "You don't understand! You never listen!"

"I'm glad that I could help," Mr. Scott thought with stinging sarcasm.

With a heart full of lead, he trudged out to his sanctuary... the garage. Unlike most days, it provided no peace. There was no solace in his saws, no satisfaction in his screwdrivers, and no happiness in his hammers. Even his new table saw left him troubled. "Oh," he thought, "if I could just figure out how those kids tick? Life would be so much easier if they just came with a repair manual."

The very next day he found himself in the principal's office. It'd been a long time since he'd visited, but it still elicited the same sort of visceral, gut-vibrating reaction it did when he was a kid. Now the butterflies bumping around in his innards had to do with his son's misbehavior...instead of his own.

Ms. Skinner was more than diplomatic, "We're so thankful that you were available to meet with us about Sammy. I know it's got to be hard to hear some of these things."

"Yeah," Mr. Scott nodded with embarrassment, "I'm really sorry that he's causing so much trouble in class."

Mr. Painter the principal piped up, "Sam's a good kid. He's got a good heart and wants to do the right thing. There are just a couple things that keep causing him problems."

"Let me guess," interrupted Mr. Scott. "He doesn't think he has to do anything unless he's paid for it...and he's too busy talking to his buddies to pay attention."

It'd been a long, long time since Mr. Painter had heard a parent nail things down so tightly. "So...this is something you are seeing at home, too?"

"I wish it wasn't," Mr. Scott answered, "but I guess I have to admit that I'm a big part of the problem. For years his mother has been harping on me to stop buying him everything he wants. I just hoped that buying him the stuff would make him more motivated to work harder for nice things."

Ms. Skinner was speechless.

Mr. Painter paused...and asked, "So your wife has a plan for working on this problem?"

"Yeah," Mr. Scott answered. "I really hate to admit it, but it's probably a good one. She's been saying 'no' a lot more often. You know...setting more limits with the kids about what she buys them. She's also been having them volunteer with her...so that they can see that it feels good to do good things. She's been reading this book called Love and Logic or something."

Recovering from her shock, Ms. Skinner said, "I'm so thankful for your honesty. I used to do the same thing with the kids. I used to think that if I showered them with rewards, they'd want to work really hard for me. It backfired for me, too."

Mr. Painter piped in, "Yes! I know about Love and Logic. About twenty-five years ago I started taking classes from one of the founders, Jim Fay. It helped me a lot with the students at school and my kids at home."

Mr. Scott was surprised. "Really? It's been around that long?"

"Oh, yeah, "Mr. Painter answered. "When my daughter Lori was thirteen, she was going through some of the same things. It was like she had to share a brain with all of her friends. If one of them thought or did something, she had to do it, too."

Chuckling, Mr. Scott agreed, "Yeah, it's like Sammy does everything that that Jamerson kid does."

"My wife and I really started to worry about that with Lori," Mr. Painter continued. "We started worrying that she was going to get herself in some really big trouble if she didn't learn how to resist peer pressure."

The third "E" of Love and Logic stand for Education. As we learned early in this book, kids aren't born with all of the skills they'll need for success in life. Resisting peer pressure is one of these skills! If our kids fail to learn it, they'll be destined for failure. How will they become self-managers if they're blown off course by every whim and fancy of their peers? Employers are desperate for employees who know how to do what's right even when it's not what's popular. America urgently needs citizens who do the same!

Employers are desperate for employees who know how to do what's right even when it's not what's popular. America urgently needs citizens who do the same!

Before we see how this third "E" of Love and Logic applies to teaching this skill, let's review what we've learned so far.

In Chapter 1...

- Patty learned that she couldn't assume that her daughter knew how to get ready in the morning until she'd taken the time to show her.
- Patty also learned that great educators model skills, provide visual cues, ask plenty of guiding questions, and let their students practice when the consequences of foul-ups are small.
- Two-year-old Shelby's learned how to dine with dignity when her parents used modeling, visual cues, guiding questions, and plenty of practice.

In Chapter 2, Mr. Hammer...

- apologized to his son, Max, for robbing him of opportunities to see that he had what it takes to solve problems.
- learned that it's far easier to educate our kids when they're calm and we are, too.
- applied five steps to help Max learn how to solve his problems with a demanding coach.

In Chapter 3, Ruby discovered...

- that most of how we think and feel is learned.
- that we all have the power to choose happiness.
- how to apply the five steps used by Max's dad to help her kids learn positive mental habits.

In Chapter 4, Liz and Lester learned...

- that endless explaining is not the best way to educate our kids.

- how to teach by sharing information about possible consequences and then allowing their kids to make the mistake anyway.
- that this enables our kids to see how wise we are.

In Chapter 5, I met a recovering Helicopter mom who...

- described how she parked across the street from her daughter's school to quickly rescue her from any peer-related problems.
- learned to empower her daughter with skills rather than cripple her with rescuing.
- realized that there's no greater gift than the self-esteem associated with knowing that we can solve the problems we encounter.

Now let's see how Mr. Scott used this third "E" to help his kids become steady oaks rather than tumbling tumbleweeds.

"I just wish that kids came with an owner's manual," Mr. Scott lamented. "You know what I'm saying?"

Mr. Painter agreed, "I hear you! They can humble the strongest and most intelligent adults. Now...I have to say...Love and Logic is about the closest thing I've ever found to that manual you're talking about." Handing Mr. Scott a sheet of paper, he continued, "Here's a handout that really helped my wife and I."

LOVE AND LOGIC TIPS FOR HELPING KIDS RESIST PEER PRESSURE

- *Don't be afraid to say "no."*
  One way that kids learn to say "no" to their friends is by hearing us say "no" to them.

186

- *Talk only when both of you are in a good mood.*
  Never try to talk with a child who's angry or frustrated.

- *Share love and concern rather than telling them what to do.*
  We can't control what our kids do when we aren't around.
  In fact, parents who try often end up encouraging their kids
  to rebel.

  When we share our love, as well as our concern about how
  certain friends and decisions might affect their lives, they're
  far more likely to listen.

- *Say, "You get to decide whether you let others run your life or
  whether you take charge of it yourself."*
  This simple statement shares control and helps kids begin
  thinking about whether they want to be leaders or followers.

- *Encourage them to use you as the "bad guy."*
  Kids often find it easier to say "no" to their friends when
  they're encouraged to say something like, "The last time I
  did something like that my parents went psychotic. They're
  so crazy that you don't know what they might do. They have
  spies everywhere."

- *Thank them and end the talk with high expectations.*
  Say, "Thanks for listening! Your friends are lucky to have
  someone like you who knows right from wrong!"

Mr. Scott was guardedly optimistic, "This really helped?"

Mr. Painter nodded, "It didn't solve all of our problems, but it
gave us a way of talking about the subject without getting into
nasty arguments. The hardest part for my wife and I was coming to grips with the fact that we couldn't choose our daughter's
friends. That was hard!"

Ms. Skinner agreed. "I don't have kids of my own, but I remember when my mom tried to lecture me about the types of friends I shouldn't have. As soon as the words came out of her mouth, I found myself wanting to hang out with them even more. I think if she would have just talked with me, instead of trying to boss me around, things would have gone a lot better."

"So I shouldn't go home and tell Sammy to stay away from that Jamerson character?" Mr. Scott joked.

Mr. Painter laughed, "Bingo!"

After getting a bit of coaching from Mr. Painter, Dad walked out of that school with a smile on his face and a little bit of hope. That evening, he pulled the handout out of his pocket, unfolded it, and showed it to his wife.

With grace beyond comprehension, she resisted the urge to rub salt in his wounds by saying, "I told you so!" Instead, she smiled and asked, "Do you think this is something that you're going to try?"

Appreciating her tact, he replied, "I've got to do something. Anything has got to work better than what I've been doing. And you're right. You know how much I hate to admit that you're right. I really do need to stop buying them everything they want. I thought it would make them more motivated to achieve something with their lives. Now that I see how snobby and de-manding it's made them I feel sick to my stomach."

Over the past three decades, we've seen far too many parents, like Mr. Scott, who've believed that the key to motivating their kids was to buy them lots of expensive stuff. As strange as it may seem, their logic goes something like the following:

If my kid has a lot of really nice luxuries, then they will want to continue this sort of lifestyle as an adult. Since they will want this sort of lifestyle, they will work really hard in school so that they can someday afford it.

WRONG!

There are few things that create more unhappiness, disrespect, and lack of self-control than being given everything you want without having to earn it. Like many well-meaning parents, Mr. Scott had to learn this the hard way. Since his kids were so deeply angry, it took quite a while before he found the right time to start educating them about resisting peer pressure.

There are few things that create more unhappiness, disrespect, and lack of self-control than being given everything you want without having to earn it.

At 65 miles per hour, Dad decided that this was a good time to start. Sammy was captive in the passenger seat, and he actually seemed to be in a good mood for a change. Remembering his coaching session with Mr. Painter, he resisted the urge to leap into a lecture about how his son shouldn't hang out with those "bad" kids. Instead, he locked in the love, "I love you, son."

Sammy was a bit weirded-out! "Uh...yeah...Dad."

Mr. Scott continued, "I love you so much that I've made the mistake of trying to boss you around about your friends."

"Dad, this is really kind of weird," Sammy replied.

Dad agreed, "I know, but I just want you to know that I'm going to work really hard on being better about that."

Sammy was silent.

Remembering a great line he learned from Mr. Painter, Dad forged on, "Can I share something that concerns me...just as long as I don't tell you what to do about it?"

"Uh, I guess so," mumbled his son.

"I'm worried," continued Dad, "that you might be letting others run your life instead of taking charge of it yourself."

"Awe, Dad!" Sammy complained. "I'm fine."

Sidestepping an argument, Dad replied, "That's good. I won't hassle you about it then. I just know how hard it is for adults to say no to their friends."

"It's not a big deal," sighed Sammy.

"Good," Dad smiled. "I just want to do a better job of helping...rather than bossing you around. Let me know if there is anything I can do to help."

"It's not so hard for me," Sammy replied.

Resisting the urge to say what he was really thinking, Dad continued with the plan. "That's great. If you ever feel really pressured to do the wrong thing, you have my permission to tell them how crazy and psychotic I am."

Sammy liked this part! "Yeah, so you just want me to tell them the truth."

"Very funny," Dad chuckled. "Seriously, it's just fine with me if you say something like, 'My dad is so crazy and psychotic that you never know what he'd do if he found out. I can't take a chance.'"

"For real?" Sammy smiled.

"You bet," Dad nodded. "If that'll get you off the hook with your friends, you can use it anytime. It won't hurt my feelings."

"Uh...okay," Sammy replied, "but I still think this is sort of weird."

Dad agreed, "Yeah, I bet it feels that way. I just appreciate you listening. Your friends are really lucky to have someone like you...someone who knows right from wrong. Just let me know how I can help."

"Uh...okay," Sammy repeated.

"One more thing," Dad added. "I hope you let me know if I ever try to boss you around about this stuff again. Because I love you so much, I might slip. Just say, 'Dad, you're starting to get bossy.' That'll help me a lot."

Although it's unlikely that this little talk with save Sammy from all of his peer-related problems, it's opened the door for better communication between him and his dad. It's also improved the odds that he'll actually come to his father for help when the pressure really gets tough.

Experience

The Scott sibs were becoming less enthused about Love and Logic each day. Their lifestyle had declined precipitously since their dear mother learned about it. To make matters even worse, their once-wonderful father had also jumped on the bandwagon. Now, both of their parents were saying horrible things like:

- *Sure…you can have those $200 sneakers. The ones we were planning to buy you cost $35. As soon as you can come up with the other $165, they are yours.*
- *How are you planning to pay for the renewal of your cell phone service? Some kids decide to get a prepaid calling plan instead.*
- *You may wear those sorts of clothes when you are an adult and can pay for them yourself.*
- *You may either do your chores or pay a professional to do them.*

Believe it or not, Mom and Dad were even using the dreaded "n" word…"No!"

These were desperate times for the Scott sibs, and this was all too clear one day as Stevie sauntered down the mall with her pubescent pals.

"That top is so cool!" screeched Sasha.

"That one is so mine!" mouthed Maura.

"No way. Those are lame. I'm getting this one!" pointed Patrice.

"You've got to get one of these, Stevie!" they announced in unison. "Then we'd all be looking fine!"

"My parents are so five-minutes-ago," Stevie sassed sarcastically, "it's like they think I'm supposed to wear rags. They keep saying crap like, 'You can have those clothes when you're an adult.'"

"No!" Sasha screamed.

Maura just moaned.

Patrice had a plan, "Just go and ask to try it on. We'll talk to the lady so that she won't have a chance to watch. Just put it on under your shirt and walk out. She'll be too busy to notice anything."

Stevie was scared, "Yeah, but what if I get caught?"

"Don't be so paranoid," pressured Patrice. "It's not like it's such a big deal. I do it all of the time. Just put it on under your shirt and walk out."

With hands on their hips and heads a-swaying, Maura and Sasha turned up the heat, "We didn't now you were such a baby."

That afternoon, Mrs. Scott received a phone call…from the police station.

Stevie was one of the lucky ones! She got caught the very first time! She had the great fortune of learning a critical life lesson when she was still a juvenile…and the "price tag" of her mistake was still relatively small. Many aren't so lucky. They either get away with their crime…or they have parents who bail them out of the consequences of their criminal behavior.

Sadly, many fail to learn until they are hired by some un-suspecting employer. Their resumes look good, they have no criminal record, and they're charming. All goes well until they get promoted to positions of greater trust. Then the tempta-tion becomes too great. There are just too many opportunities to "skim a little off of the top" or to make a little on the side by bending the rules.

Making matters worse, most of these individuals have never learned to live within any sort of financial limits. Since they lack any understanding of wise financial stewardship, they spend…

and spend…and spend! When their financial woes begin to catch up with them, and they experience an acute sense of desperation, the temptation reaches epic proportions. Then they make headlines…

- TELECOM CEO FUNDS LAVISH LIFESYLE WITH COMPANY CASH
- CHIEF CONTROLLER FOUND GUILTY OF EMBEZZLEMENT
- CHURCH VOLUNTEER CASHES IN ON THE COLLECTION PLATE

The fourth "E" of Love and Logic stands for Experience. Some kids seem far too stubborn to learn the easy way. They seem oblivious to our good example, unfazed by our high expectations, and unwilling to accept the education we offer. Yes! These are the youngsters affectionately referred to as "strong willed." They test our patience, humble our hearts, and learn only by experiencing the consequences of their bad behavior. It's as if they learn life's most important lessons from the inside-out…rather than the outside-in. Only when they're fortunate enough to make afford-able mistakes, and have parents who love them enough to hold them accountable, will they gain the wisdom they need to survive in today's complicated and dangerous world.

Before we see how the fourth "E" applies to Stevie Scott's shoplifting saga, let's review what we've learned so far…

In Chapter 1, June learned that…

- strong-willed children often have to learn the hard way by making plenty of mistakes…and experiencing the conse-quences associated with them.

- it's far better for kids to learn by making plenty of small mistakes when they are young than life-and-death ones when they are older.
- by spending too much time nagging, reminding, or warning, she was robbing her daughter Patty of affordable learning opportunities.

In Chapter 2, Mr. and Mrs. Hammer...

- learned that how they respond to their son's successes is just as important as how they react to his mistakes.
- realized that using excessive praise can create kids who believe that being smart and doing everything really well is more important than learning and trying things that are difficult.
- used a three-step process for helping Max gradually understand that hard work and perseverance is more important than high intelligence, handouts, or luck.

In Chapter 3, Ruby realized...

- that our kids can develop negative thinking habits if they experience more of our attention when they are miserable than when they are content.
- how negative attention can be just as rewarding as positive.
- that she needed to make a systematic effort to emotionally connect with her kids when they were happy...and to hand the problem back when they weren't.

In Chapter 4, Liz and Larry...

- struggled with the habit of rubbing salt in the wounds by lecturing their tots after they made mistakes.

- learned that saying, "I told you this would happen," "Are you going to do that again?" or "I hope you learned your lesson!" was making it tougher for their kids to learn from their mistakes.
- discovered that great wisdom comes from experiencing the consequences of our poor decisions…not from being lectured about them.

In Chapter 5, Lester Leisureman learned…

- that he was crippling his twenty-three-year old son Lex by allowing him to live at home and mooch off of him.
- how to kick Lex out of the house…in a very loving way.
- when we do the right thing by expecting our kids to experience responsibility, there will be no shortage of folks who'll criticize us for being mean.

Now let's see how the Scotts survived daughter Stevie's shoplifting saga. Mom was beet red as she held the receiver to her ear. On the other end of the line, tears gushed out of Stevie's eyes. Between sobs, sniffs, and snorts, she begged, "Mom. I am so sorry. I don't know what I was thinking. I'll never do anything like that again. It was just that I…well…I really wanted it so bad. All of my friends….they were getting them…and I just…I just…I don't know."

Mom was too angry to speak.

Stevie continued, "Mom! You need to come get me. I'm so sorry. I don't know what I was thinking."

Mom was still too angry to speak.

"Mom! Mom. Mom? Are you there?" Stevie asked, "Why aren't you saying anything?"

Suddenly, a little voice from Love and Logic crept into Mom's mind, "When you don't know what to do, or you are too angry to think straight, delay the consequence."

Before she could speak, that little voice repeated itself, "When you don't know what to do, or you are too angry to think straight, delay the consequence."

"Why aren't you saying anything?" Stevie repeated.

"I'm too angry to talk right now," Mom informed through clenched teeth, "There are a number of things I need to do this afternoon, so it's going to be quite a while before I can get down there."

"Mom!" Stevie screamed in disbelief. "You need to get down here now!"

"Here's the deal, Stevie," Mom replied. "I promise that if I ever end up in jail, I won't expect you to drop everything and bail me out at a moment's notice. I'll be down as soon as I've had a chance to do the things I'd planned on."

When you don't know what to do, or you are too angry to think straight, delay the consequence.

As she hung up the phone, Mrs. Scott felt like the worst mother in the world. She could have dropped everything and run down to the police station, but somehow that seemed the wrong thing to do. Despite all of her guilt and sadness, she still believed that Stevie would be far better off in the long term if she had to cool her heels for a while in the slammer. She kept reminding herself, "Love and Logic teaches that kids are done no favors when their parents rescue them from the consequences of their poor decisions."

She had to hold the phone away from her ear as her loving husband reacted to the news.

"She's where? She did what?" he screamed. "When I get my hands on that kid…"

Mrs. Scott agreed, "I know, honey. I'm so mad that I can't see straight…but I have a plan."

"Huh?" he responded.

"Let's take our time getting down there," she replied. "That way she can get a little taste of what happens when you land yourself in jail. It'll also give us some time to think and figure out what to say."

"But she's probably going to need to go to court," he interrupted.

"I hope so," she added.

"Yeah, but then she's going to need a lawyer," he blurted. "How are we going to afford that?"

"I don't think we have to," she replied.

With obvious irritation, he countered, "If she doesn't have a good lawyer, she's not going to stand a chance in court!"

Mrs. Scott was simply too angry to use Love and Logic with her hovering hubby. "What are you thinking? Do you think it's a good thing for her to get off the hook on this? Do you think it's going to do any good to bail her out? That's why she's in the jam in the first place. Every time she gets herself in trouble, you make sure that everything is just smoothed over. If that's what you want, you'll have to do it without my help!"

On rare occasions, it's really good not to use Love and Logic with the ones we love. Yep! You read that correctly. Sometimes it's more effective to let loose than to hold back...that is, only when this reaction comes as a total surprise to the other person and we avoid attacking with hurtful names or put-downs.

On a daily basis, Mrs. Smith was predictably soft-spoken and empathetic. Since this was the case, her sudden change of demeanor had a massive impact on her husband. If, in contrast, her daily demeanor was dictatorial and loud, her husband would have tuned her out.

"That's not what I want," he wept. "I just don't want her to think that we don't care."

"I know," she agreed with love in her voice. "I don't want that either, but I know that she has to face the music."

Mr. and Mrs. Scott aren't any different than most of us. We all want our kids to know how much we love them, and we all worry that letting them experience consequences will somehow damage our relationship with them. This is a valid concern! Nothing's more important than our kids knowing that we love them and want to help. That's why Love and Logic draws a distinction between three types of parental responses:

- Standing *beside* our kids
- Standing *between* our kids
- Standing *against* our kids

"Standing beside our kids" means that we allow them to experience the consequences of their actions while giving them plenty of love, moral support, and suggestions. The goal of this reaction is to help the child learn.

"Standing between our kids" means that we insulate and rescue them from experiencing the consequences of their actions. In other words, we stand between them and the real world consequences of their decisions. The goal of this reaction is to meet the adult's need to feel like a hero.

"Standing against our kids" means that we add insult to injury by yelling, threatening, laying on guilt trips, or trying to provide additional arbitrary punishments. The goal of this reaction is to punish or get even with the child.

Most readers can guess which reaction is the Love and Logic brand! Parents who understand this approach are always willing to stand beside their children as they cope with consequences. If Mr. and Mrs. Scott intend to help their daughter learn the maximum life lesson from this experience, this reaction has got to be their goal.

Late that evening, they drove to the police station...very slowly. They took their time walking up the steps, and they reminded themselves not to rush as they described the situation to the attending officer. As Stevie walked into the conference room, wearing her new bracelets, they threw their arms around her and said, "Oh Stevie. We love you. This has got to be a horrible problem to have."

Stevie would have found the situation far more comfortable if her mother and father had yelled. Instead, their empathy and concern hit her like a ton of lead. Have you ever wished that someone was angry at you...rather than sad?

Stevie hunched over the table with her head in her hands, "I'm so sorry. I don't know what I was thinking. It was just that my friends...well they...I don't know."

Mom was ready! She'd rehearsed all of the way down to the station, "Oh, we'd be really mad at you if you did something that landed us in jail...but this is your life. How does it make any sense for us to be angry at you for messing up your life?"

"I don't know!" Stevie moaned.

Now it was Dad's turn. Remembering his wife's wonderful outburst, he said, "Do you have a plan for how you are going to handle your court appearance?"

"You could get me a lawyer," Stevie answered with hope in her voice.

"I'd get the best lawyer in town," Dad answered, "if I were the one who was facing this situation. Here's the problem. You're the one who's facing this situation. Do you have any money to hire one?"

Stevie had turned from mournful to mad, "Dad! How can you say that? If you loved me you wouldn't even joke about that."

With great love in her voice, Mom replied, "Oh, honey. Your Dad and I aren't joking. If you'd like some ideas about how to solve this problem, just let us know."

Stevie didn't say a word as she rode home with her parents. Her head spun as she tried to get a grip on what she was going to do. Since the juvenile courts were backed up for weeks, she'd have plenty of time to consider the possibilities, "Maybe they'll lock me up...or maybe probation...How am I going to pay for my lawyer? Maybe the judge will just give me another chance... no, they don't do that...maybe they do. What about cheerleading tryouts? Why did I do such a stupid thing?"

Stevie was already getting some wonderful practice for life! As we all know, the world is becoming ever more complex and challenging. If our kids are going to survive and thrive, they're going to need plenty of "thinking practice" before they get there. While none of us hopes that our children make the errors committed by sweet Stevie, such blunders need not lead to a life of crime and desperation. If we stand beside them, and allow them to cope with the problem using their own brain power, we dramatically up the odds that they'll gain wonderful wisdom...and life skills...from the experience.

If our kids are going to survive and thrive, they're going to need plenty of "thinking practice" before they get there.

As they walked in the house, Dad patted her on the back and said, "I'm really sorry that you're going through this. I'm really disappointed with what you did, but I will always love you the same. If you are interested in any ideas about what you might do, just let me know."

There's great hope for Stevie! Over the past three decades, we've met countless parents who've been through similar situations with their youngsters. Those who've stood behind their kids typically look back and say, "Getting caught and having to go to court was the very best thing that ever happened to my child!"

Empathy

Lisa lives at 101 Lilac Lane, Lenny lives across the street at 102, and Lyle resides at 103. Like most youngsters, each devotes some of their weekly schedule to being irresponsible…and a bit of it to being downright naughty.

When Lisa complains, "Why didn't you wash my favorite shirt?" her mother replies…

"Oh, honey. This is sad. I wash clothes that kids put in the hamper for me."

When Lenny complains the same, his mother answers…

"Why do I always have to remind you to put your clothes in the hamper? Okay, I'll hand wash it for you, but it's going to take some time to dry."

When Lyle does, his mother barks…

"I am sick and tired of having to pick up after you!"

When Lisa forgets to do her chores, her dad sadly informs…

"Lisa, this is such a drag. I'd love to take you over to your friends, but I've spent all afternoon doing your chores."

When Lenny forgets his domestic duties, his dad dodges the issue…

"There are a lot of things that you need to do around here, but I'll take you if you promise to get caught up later this week."

When Lyle drops the ball on his chores, his father hammers...

"This makes me so mad! You aren't going to leave this house until every single one of those chores is done! I mean it!"

When Lisa gets in trouble at school, Mom and Dad counsel...

"Oh, Lisa, it sounds like you've really got yourself in trouble. If you want some ideas about how to solve this problem, let us know."

When Lenny's on the hot seat with his teachers, his mother and father assure...

"I don't know why they have all of those silly rules, anyway. We'll have a talk with your teacher. Don't worry about it, sweetie. We'll take care of it."

Whey Lyle's in trouble, there's no doubt that his parents are perturbed...

"That's it! You are in big trouble, Mister! You are going to sit down this weekend and write your teacher a letter, telling her how sorry you are! You are NOT going to leave this house! We hope this teaches you a lesson!"

Lisa's parents understand that the healthiest children grow up with parents who stand right beside them when things go wrong. Although they know that she needs to experience the consequences of her actions, they also understand that she'll only learn from them if she isn't spending all of her time feeling angry and resentful. Deep in their hearts, they know that their sweet daughter will only grow to become a respectful, responsible, and self-controlled adult if they leave her believing that they are on her side…even when she has to experience the pain of her problems. As a result, Lisa walks around most of the time thinking…

When I mess up, it makes my life really sad…but people still care about me. I'd better think about the consequences of my decisions.

Because Lenny's parents love him, too, they want the very best for him. Unfortunately, they're tragically mistaken about how to give it to him. Standing between him and the consequences of his actions, they leave him thinking…

I'm so special that rules, limits, or any sort of boundaries don't apply. I'm entitled to royal treatment!

Lyle's parents love him just as much. Obviously, their definition of "love" is much different than their neighbors'. Because they desperately want their son to learn the difference between right and wrong, they bark orders, show him how upset they are, and punish. Although they don't intend to, they're standing against him and the world. Because of this, he walks around thinking…

When I mess up, it really makes other people mad. Next time, I'd better not get caught. One of these days I won't have to put up with this crap. Then I'll get what I deserve!

Lisa, Lenny, and Lyle each have parents who love them very much and want the best for them. Nevertheless, each will grow up with a very different view of the world and their place within it. Consider the following questions:

- As adults, which one of these young people would you rather have working for you?
- Which one would you feel the most comfortable with doing your bookkeeping?
- Which would you prefer to have as a son- or daughter-in-law?
- Which would you vote for to run our country?

Here are some additional thoughts to ponder:

- Which stand the greatest chance of becoming corporate criminals?
- Which will be the most likely to accept bribes and do favors for those who treat them special?
- Which will be more prone to cheat on their spouses?
- Which is most likely to remain a person of high integrity and moral character when they aren't being watched and temptations run high?

Lisa's got the clear advantage on the neighbor kids! Why? Simply because she doesn't believe that she's entitled to special treatment, she doesn't believe that she has to lie, steal, or cheat to get what she wants, and she understands that she must remain responsible for the consequences of her actions.

Lisa's biggest advantage is that she truly cares about others. When we raise kids who do, their internal rule system keeps them on the straight and narrow. They become adults who self-manage because they care about how their behavior affects those around them. The future of our great nation rests entirely on our ability to raise more kids with this quality. Why? Because there will never be enough laws, police officers, or prisons if we don't. A country cannot survive long on external regulations when its citizens lack internal ones.

A country cannot survive long on external regulations when its citizens lack internal ones.

The fifth "E" of Love and Logic stands for Empathy. There's a strong connection between this essential skill and self-control. Before looking at this link, let's review.

In Chapter 1, Mr. and Mrs. Thomas...

- learned that consequences provided with empathy enable kids to learn from their mistakes, while consequences with anger allow them to blame us for the problem.
- found out that this empathy must be delivered before the consequence...not afterwards.
- applied a time-tested technique that allowed them to remain empathetic and calm as they taught their son how to do his chores without reminders and without pay.

In Chapter 2, Mike's mother...

- realized that she was parenting just like her mother...with plenty of anger.
- learned how to change this habit by memorizing just one simple empathetic statement.
- stayed ever so sweet as she described to Mike how he would need to repay her for all of the time she had used talking to his teacher about his misbehavior.

In Chapter 3, Ruby realized that...

- her children had developed the "no sense in both of us worrying about this" syndrome.
- this happens when we use sympathy rather than empathy.

- sympathy means that we make our children's problems our own, while empathy means that we show genuine concern while handing their problems back.

In Chapter 4, we saw…

- how it's normal to have great difficulty displaying sincere empathy when you are angry with your kids.
- why it's okay to delay the consequence by saying, "I'm so angry that I can't think straight. I make better decisions when I'm calm. I'll do something about this later."
- that delayed consequences work with difficult adults, too.

In Chapter 5, Lonnie learned…

- that when she used empathy with her husband, he was better equipped to avoid bailing out his responsibility-deficit-disordered son.
- how empathy allows others to think and problem-solve with their frontal cortex, rather than reacting with their brain stem.
- why empathy is good for marriages, too.

Now let's examine the critical connection between using empathy with our kids and teaching them self-control. A good place to start is by going back in time and taking a look at the world during the late 1930's and 1940's. At this time, peace-loving people were reeling with disbelief and dismay over the events taking place in Nazi Germany and across Europe. How was it possible that so many seemingly ordinary people could be willing parties to genocide? How was it that so many could be drawn into committing such horrific acts? How was it that so many appeared to abandon any sort of internal moral compass in favor of following the leadership of such a mad and evil man?

Many great thinkers of the time sought to understand…and hopefully prevent something like this from ever happening again. A brilliant scientist named Kurt Lewin devised an experiment to examine the effects of different political and social systems on human behavior.1 To do this, Lewin and his colleagues created three separate experimental groups. In each group, leaders managed groups of children, with a very specific leadership style.

One experimental group was managed by adults with a laissez-faire approach. These adults set very few limits, essentially allowing the children to do as they pleased.

A second group was led by adults with an authoritarian approach. These adults barked orders and demonstrated absolute authority. The complete opposite of the laissez-faire teachers, they demonstrated little concern for their students and allowed no decision-making.

A final group was led by adults using a democratic leadership style. These leaders allowed the children generous freedom for decision-making, while maintaining order through necessary limits. The more responsible the kids behaved, the more choices they were allowed to make.

The results where interesting. Which children worked the hardest? Which completed the most work? Which groups appeared to run the smoothest with the least amount of bickering and fighting? Those run by adults using an authoritarian approach. Yes! The groups managed by those uncaring, dictator-like folks came out on top.

That's as long as those adults were there to bark their orders.

Lewin and his colleagues weren't surprised, and they weren't all that interested. What aroused their curiosity far more was how the children would behave when the adult was absent…and they were free to do as they pleased.

Children in the laissez -faire group remained just as out of control as they'd been when the adults were in the room. In homes where parents use this approach, there really isn't much difference between the lack of structure when they are home and the lack of structure when they aren't.

Children in the authoritarian-managed group went bonkers the very moment the adult stepped out of the room. They did little or no work, and displayed far more aggressive behavior. Have you ever seen this happen with parents who try to employ this approach? Have you ever met a child who was so dependent upon external control that they couldn't handle even a dewdrop of freedom? Have you ever seen kids who look perfect...until they go off to their first year of college?

The children in the democratic-led groups were the only ones capable of behaving when the adults were absent. Because they were acquainted with freedom on a daily basis, they weren't like ships without rudders when they suddenly received more of it. The goal of Love and Logic parenting is to give our kids so much practice with small freedoms when they are small that they can handle bigger ones when they are older.

> **The goal of Love and Logic parenting is to give our kids so much practice with small freedoms when they are small that they can handle bigger ones when they are older.**

Lewin and his colleagues concluded two things from these results:

- The ability to handle freedom is learned. Those who never have it, or have it without equal doses of responsibility, suffer great difficulty managing their own behavior.
- Human beings are like mechanical springs. The harder they're compressed by external forces, the more they'll rebound when these forces are absent.

So, what does all of this have to do with the fifth "E" of Love and Logic, Empathy? Do authoritarian, dictatorial parents communicate it? It doesn't take a research study to see that such parents fail to meet this universal human emotional need! Can you imagine growing up without understanding that the most important adults in your life love you even when you're acting not-so-lovable? Can you imagine feeling like your parents care nothing about your ideas and your choices? Unfortunately, many folks know exactly how this feels. When this sense of deprivation becomes severe enough, deep-seated feelings of entitlement exist. Like Lyle at 103 Lilac Lane, they count the days until they can take what they've never had. "Who cares if somebody gets hurt in the process?" they reason. "The world owes me because my life has been so dismal."

Do laissez-faire parents communicate empathy? At first glance it may seem so. Upon closer inspection it's clear that they don't. Laissez-faire parents communicate sympathy. Sympathy leaves people dependent, whereas empathy leaves them empowered.

Empathy also provides inherent limits. While establishing compassion, it communicates to our children that they are ultimately responsible for coping with the consequences of their decisions. Since the children of laissez-faire parents lack both empathy and limits, they also develop a deep-seated sense of entitlement. Like Lenny at 102 Lilac Lane, they believe, "The world owes me because I'm so special."

Isn't it interesting...yet very sad...that two seemingly counter-opposite styles of parenting create the very same result?

Love and Logic parents are essentially democratic parents. While allowing plenty of decision-making when potential consequences are small, they retain firm control over the major decisions affecting the family. Through this, their actions communicate a strong dose of empathy. Each and every day, this unspoken message rings clear...

- *We care enough about you to let you practice for the real world.*
- *We love you so much that we'll allow you to make decisions that help you learn about this world.*
- *We adore you enough to set limits and make the decisions you are unable or not ready to make.*
- *We love you and our country so much that we are passionately dedicated to teaching you that freedom is not free...that when you abuse it, you lose it.*

Lisa at 101 Lilac Lane is a lucky little girl!

Thank you for reading this book. Thank you for loving your kids. Thank you for doing your part to raise the types of kids that employers really want...and America desperately needs!

---

1 Lewin, K., Lippit, R. and White, R.K. (1939). Patterns of aggressive behavior in experimentally created social climates. Journal of Social Psychology, 10, 271-301.

INDEX